PEOPLE
WHO
LED TO
MY
PLAYS

PEOPLE WHO LED TO MY PLAYS

Adrienne Kennedy

Theatre Communications Group

People Who Led to My Plays is published by Theatre Communications Group, Inc., 520 Eighth Avenue, 24th Floor, New York, NY 10018-4156

Published by arrangement with Alfred A. Knopf, Inc.

This publication is made possible in part by the New York State Council on the Arts with the support of Governor Andrew Cuomo and the New York State Legislature.

TCG books are exclusively distributed to the book trade by Consortium Book Sales and Distribution.

Cataloging-in-Publication Data is on file at the Library of Congress.

ISBN 978-1-55936-125-5 (paperback)

Cover design by Susan Mitchell

First paperback edition, September 1988
Third printing, January 2016

This book is dedicated
to my mother and father,
Etta and C. W. Hawkins,
my sons, Adam and Joe,
and Joseph Kennedy

Acknowledgments

I would like to acknowledge the encouragement of several people . . . Janie and James S. Kennedy, Lynne Hawkins, Edward Albee, Gillian Walker Maysles, and Alice Hawkins . . . and the inspiration of my brother, Cornell Hawkins. I owe a tremendous debt to many writers and theatre people for their support and friendship and wish to thank them. I'd also like to thank Robert Gottlieb and my editor, Alice Quinn, who encouraged me to continue with the book after seeing half of its pages, giving me the confidence to pursue and finish it.

A.K.

ELEMENTARY SCHOOL
1 9 3 6 – 1 9 4 3

Fairy tales
My family
The radio
Jesus
My teachers
The movies, dolls, paper dolls
Hitler
JANE EYRE

More and more often as my plays are performed in colleges and taught in universities, people ask me why I write as I do, who influenced me. When they ask this they are usually referring to my original one-act plays, *Funnyhouse of a Negro*, *The Owl Answers*, *A Rat's Mass* and *A Movie Star Has to Star in Black and White*, and not to the commissioned work I've done in the last decade for Juilliard (*Electra* and *Orestes*), the Mark Taper Forum (*The Life of Robert Johnson*), or the Empire State Youth Institute (*Chaplin's Childhood*). But they do continue to ask. Who influenced you to write in such a nonlinear way? Who are your favorite playwrights?

After I attempt to answer, naming this playwright or that one, as time progresses I realize I never go back far enough to the beginning. So I decided to.

People on Old Maid cards (1936, age five):
Through make-believe one could control people on a small scale.

Paper dolls:
You could invent enchantment with paper.

THE BLUE BIRD (1940 movie):
Somewhere, if I could find them, there were some steps, many, many steps, that led to the Blue Bird of Happiness. But I would have to climb them and they sort of sat just in the middle of the sky. It would be worth it, though. I wondered if they were in another city. What city?

Jack and Jill:
Went up a hill to fetch a pail of water. Jack fell down and broke his crown and Jill came tumbling after. What's a crown? I asked my mother. His *head*, she said.

Blondine:
A heroine in a fairy tale who went through trials and hectic adventures to find happiness, until she befriended a tortoise who helped her destroy her nemesis, a wicked king. I had never seen a tortoise and didn't know anyone who had one. I wondered if I had to confront an evil king—who would help me?

Elves:
I asked my mother, could we leave milk for the elves that came out at night?

Burglars:
They broke into our house one night when my mother and father and brother and I were asleep. One had a gun and put it to my mother's side and took her wedding ring. Then they took the cash from the dresser. My father, who was a YMCA secretary, had just gotten paid that day. The police later discovered the burglars had followed my father home from the bank and had taken a side stairway to the attic and hidden there until almost midnight.

Goldilocks and the Three Bears, Cinderella, Jack and the Beanstalk, Little Red Riding Hood, Hansel and Gretel, The Pied Piper of Hamelin:
There was a world that existed where unusual terror reigned, a world my parents and friends couldn't reach.

Joe Louis (the heavyweight champ):
We listened to his fights on the radio. His fame and popularity crossed racial boundaries.

June and Jean:
Twins in my class in kindergarten. They walked to school on the same street as I did. I walked as close to them as possible so I could study these two people who looked exactly alike.

Miss Elbert:
She said I was the best reader in the first grade.

My mother:
Some of her sayings—
    "Every dog has their day."
    "You gotta get up before morning to fool me."
    "Don't be a greedy pig" (when, at age six, I tried to eat a whole chocolate
       cake).
    "Lord doesn't love ugly."
    "Be a lady."

Jim:
The hero of the 1930s song.

Our family:
We took drives in my father's Plymouth every Sunday (unless there was a blizzard) after dinner, which was at three o'clock . . . in the summer, fried chicken, in the winter, pork roast or roast beef. We started from Mount Pleasant, where we lived, drove out Kinsman, up Lee Road to Shaker Heights, through the winding streets of Tudor mansions. Sometimes we drove downtown to Cedar Avenue, where my father had his office at the Y. The Y had a "ballroom," a large room painted blue where I would one day have my wedding reception and where, as a teenager, I saw my father give many talks at Y banquets. Down the hall from the "ballroom" were rooms where guests at the Y stayed . . . small single bedrooms with plaid bedspreads and a desk. My brother and I peeked into the rooms that were empty. How could I or any of us know that it would be in one of these rooms where my father would spend the last days of his life, sick from emphysema, divorced from my mother and bereaved of his second wife?

    But we didn't know that then as we peeked in the rooms, and ran down the hallway to the stairway that led to the main floor and the reception room, past the office that had a plaque on the door with my father's name.

My father would greet us, rushing out of his office, smiling, and we'd climb back into the 1937 Plymouth, where my mother sat waiting.

"Let's drive by Lake Erie," we'd say, and so we would drive along the lake until it got dark. "They're going to build this lake up one day," my father always said. My mother would finally announce that we should go home. And when we got home, she, my brother and I had chilled jello with

bananas and vanilla wafers that my mother had carefully made the night before. My father smoked a cigar. I was excited and happy because soon Jack Benny would come on the radio, and we all loved Jack Benny and Eddie Anderson (Rochester).

My mother:
When we came back from the Imperial Theatre after seeing movies like *Hold Back the Dawn* or *Kitty Foyle*, she'd sit in her favorite maroon-colored chair in the corner of the living room and light a cigarette . . . a Lucky Strike . . . and talk about why she liked the movie. "When I was in school I acted in plays," she'd say wistfully.

My brother:
We swung on the big swings and the baby swings, we climbed the parallel bars and rode a chained affair called the merry-go-round. We played in the sandbox and we played baseball. And we walked to the theater every Saturday to see Hopalong Cassidy, Charlie Chan, Gloria Jean and Donald O'Connor while we ate pretzels and potato chips.

People in nursery rhymes:
Humpty Dumpty, Jack Sprat, Little Bo Peep. People did illogical things that had a deeper, more puzzling meaning.

People in fairy tales:
There was a journey in life that was dark and light, good and evil, and people were creatures of extreme love, hatred, fear, ambition and vengefulness, but there was a reward if one kept seeing the light and hoping.

Fairy tales:
Stories of people could hypnotize.

Fairies:
They waved magic wands and everything became different.

People in the Bible:
Life was old.

Comic strips—Little Orphan Annie, Blondie and Dagwood, Bringing Up Father:
Our family laughed over their doings.

People in the movies:
Whom I saw every Saturday afternoon from the time I was six to thirteen (especially Charles Boyer).

Santa Claus:
Up on the housetop, click click click; down through the chimney comes good St. Nick. He called me up once right after I came home from school and asked me what I wanted for Christmas. I wondered how Santa knew our phone number. I was eleven years old before my mother told me that "Santa" had been my father.

Sabu, Turhan Bey:
Two people in the movies who were *not* white.

A few others I saw:
Ella Fitzgerald (one movie); Pearl Bailey (one movie); Butterfly McQueen (one movie); Stepin Fetchit (many movies).

Myself:
Why did I have to wear long plaid dresses, knee socks and Buster Brown shoes? And a big bow tied at the top of my braid?

My Aunt Mary Lee often laughed at me and asked why did I stare at everyone so.

Virginia (our family friend):
One Saturday afternoon she took me downtown on the streetcar to see *The Wizard of Oz* and afterward bought me a chocolate ice cream soda, the first I'd ever had. How I loved that afternoon.

Souls, witches, magicians, Sleeping Beauty:
I hoped no one would put me to sleep for a hundred years. For when I woke up where would my parents and brother be?

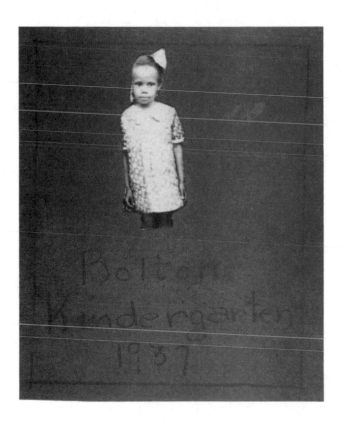

Adrienne Ames (my mother and my name):
My mother often told the story of how when she was pregnant she went to a movie and saw Adrienne Ames and decided to name me for her. How could I see then that my name was responsible for inspiring in me a curiosity about celebrity and glamour?

Mummies, monsters, the Devil:
I worried a great deal about what could happen to a person while she was asleep . . . especially since my mother made me say every single night:

"Now I lay me down to sleep.
I pray the Lord my soul to keep.
And if I die before I wake,
I pray the Lord my soul to take."

Mary, Mother of Jesus:
The most wondrous time of the school year were the weeks before Christmas. We learned all the Christmas songs: "Silent Night," "O Come, All Ye Faithful," "Up on the Housetop (Click, Click)." We read "'Twas the Night Before Christmas." We made clay presents of ashtrays and animals for our parents; we crocheted doilies for our mothers' furniture; we drew green Christmas trees and red Santas that decorated our rooms. We made Christmas cards of sleighs, bells and candy canes and took them home through the icy snow to our parents. And we put on the annual Christmas play.

In the fourth grade I was chosen to play Jesus' mother, Mary. The entire school was to come to the play. During the rehearsals in the drafty school auditorium after school I experienced a sensation which was entirely new to me. Mrs. Filetti, the teacher who planned the play, insisted that Lawrence (he played Joseph) and I believe that we were Jesus' parents on our way to Bethlehem. And that I, Mary, was about to give birth to Christ. I was told I had to faint first, then walk a little further to the manger and faint again. And then the baby Jesus would be born.

Lawrence (Joseph) had to hold my hand while we walked to Bethlehem and to hold my hand while Christ was being born and our class sang. I had told Mrs. Filetti that I didn't want to be in the school play, but she had insisted, saying I was just the right size. And how glad I was she had insisted: I got to wear a white robe, and walk off the stage accompanied by music, carrying the baby Jesus. And I sat in the hall the rest of the afternoon in my costume at the school Christmas party. Everyone talked to me. I had never received so much attention. I felt flushed and thrilled.

Jesus:
The miniature photographs and gilt-edged cards of Jesus that the church gave us in Sunday school hypnotized me. The colors, the crimsons, blues, golds . . . the black of Jesus' eyes. "Jesus loves you," Sunday school teachers repeated every Sunday, winter, spring and summer. "Jesus loves all the little boys and girls." I saved the pictures of this Jesus into whose feet they had driven nails but who arose. And who loved me.

"Negroes":
We were underdogs, and underdogs must fight in life.

Mrs. Miniver (1942 movie):
The movie, which I saw at age eleven, with Greer Garson as Mrs. Miniver, showed me that I had a desire for drama! My best friend Barbara Ann and I had a fight over who would play Mrs. Miniver in our version of the movie that would take place in Barbara's backyard with all the kids on our street. We finally decided that she would play Mrs. Miniver in the first half and I would play her in the second half.

My brother Cornell:
From the early days of *Jack Armstrong*, *Tom Mix* and *Little Orphan Annie* to

the later ones of *I Love a Mystery* and *Jack Benny*, we sat side by side next to the Philco radio and listened to the shows and then played games acting out the characters. We sent away for rings, maps and puzzles.

As a child my brother Cornell was quiet, and he ran away for a few hours (when it was snowing) when he was ten. And I know there was an unseen sadness in him.

Arenzia (my next-door neighbor):
He could read sheet music and play popular songs on the piano. Together, we bought the magazines with the words to popular songs in them and we learned them.

My father:
My father saves people, I often thought. People talked of what a fine social worker he was and how many young people he had helped set in the right direction. He raised money for Y scholarships, helped the young find work and provided guidance through the Y programs.

He gave fine stirring speeches at meetings and banquets on the value of working hard for the Negro cause and helping Negro youth. He read me poetry of Negro poets and told me stories of Du Bois, Marian Anderson and Mary Bethune. He listened to me sing spirituals, which I loved, and popular songs, which I also loved.

My mother:
She told me stories of her life in Georgia, which would one day sound remarkably like the monologues spoken by the characters in my plays. She taught me the alphabet when I was three, and she taught me to read that same year. She encouraged me to compete with my Jewish, Polish, Italian and Black classmates in elementary school, and took pride in the accomplishments of my gold and silver stars. She continued to encourage me to read, and by the fifth grade I had read all the books in the school library. She shared her secret thoughts and tears over the movies she took me to see so that I learned early that there was a secret locked inside movies and songs that caused "adults" to cry, to become quiet, to reminisce. She collected photographs of her and my father's youth in Atlanta and kept them in scrapbooks so that I was able to imagine my parents as they were when they were young. She instilled in me the desire to excel.

Mrs. Filetti:
My fifth-grade teacher gave me the role of the Virgin Mary in our Christmas play, where I learned the thrill of the attention and interest that came from wearing a costume and standing onstage pretending.

Charlotte Brontë:
I read *Jane Eyre* and learned that life was to be a great journey and it was a journey that would be spelled out with love, loyalty, devotion, loneliness, madness, sacrifice and happiness, and that very life had been experienced by an English girl one century before.

Spirituals:
I learned that I belonged to a race of people who were in touch with a kingdom of spirituality and mystery beyond my visible sight.

Paul Robeson:
My father took me to hear and see him. After hearing Robeson I realized that one person could inspire many people to strength, to courage, to believing.

Freddy Jamison:
The boy I fell in love with at eight. He could talk in long funny monologues about people.

Jesus:
He could endure, and as a "Negro" I needed that quality.

God (as a child):
I thought He lived in the sky and looked over and protected me.

"White people":
They tried to hold you back. That implied a great challenge existed in life.

The minister in our church:
He spoke the sermon in a way that said there was a rage inside religion.

Dr. Benjamin Mays (president of Morehouse College):
My father introduced me to him when I was six years old. He told me Mays
was a "great man." A great man, I remember thinking, what is a great man
and why is he a great man?

My mother (1937):
I was brought to her room by a neighbor who had been in the house all
morning. My parents' door had been closed. And I was told to stay in my
room. Suddenly I heard a loud siren. My mother's door burst open, another
neighbor had been inside her room. My father came running through the
house followed by two men with a stretcher. The neighbor said, Adrienne,
your mother wants to talk to you. My mother was lying in bed, her face
wet, her hair limp. She looked like she was dying . . . the color of her skin
almost purple.

"Be a good girl," she said and the men lifted her onto a white stretcher
and carried her to a large white ambulance.

My father disappeared with them. The siren sounded and the ambulance
took my mother away. I fled to the closet in my room, closed the door and

started weeping. The neighbor made me open the door. "Your mother will be all right," she said. It was years before I learned my mother had lost a child and had almost died.

My Italian classmates:
I would sit on the front porch and watch them as they went to communion, extraordinarily beautiful in their white communion dresses, with their catechism books, their rosaries.

Mrs. Filetti:
Long before Mrs. Rosebaugh told us about Caesar, Mrs. Filetti, our music teacher, taught us Italian melodies. "Funiculi Funicula."

Leslie Howard (GONE WITH THE WIND):
He had an English accent. How wonderful!

LITTLE HOUSE ON THE PRAIRIE:
L. I. Wilder book which we read in fifth grade. Laura in her little house on the prairie, reading and talking to her family and dreaming of growing up, led a life similar to mine in the dark, long Cleveland winters.

Mr. Kuzamano:
He ran the drugstore and gave us an extra dip of ice cream on our cones.

Jesus:
Jesus loves me, this I know, for the Bible tells me so. Little ones to Him belong, they are weak, but He is strong.

People in the constellations:
Wonder.

Zombies, mummies, the Cat Woman, ghouls, ghosts, vampires, monsters, werewolves:
And Boris Karloff and Lon Chaney (the single most frightening movie monster), the Wolf Man.

Because of the Wolf Man I asked my mother many questions about what would happen to "a person" while sleeping. And I asked her these questions for a long time. The Wolf Man held a power over me. Metamorphosis and that change of identity would, twenty years later, become a theme that would dominate my writing. The characters in my plays and stories would also change personae at an alarming rate.

The people in my mother's red scrapbook:
I yearned to know them.

Dreaming of my parents as children:
Both my parents knew all the people in the red scrapbook, because my parents had known each other since they were children. My mother told me they met walking along the road near my father's house and my father said hello to her. Summers when I stayed at my grandmother's house I would sit on the steps looking at the road trying to picture my parents meeting. It was tiring, so I'd pick a peach from the huge peach tree in the yard and go back to reading *Modern Screen*.

I started to read *Modern Screen* in the summer, because the movie changed only once in the one movie theater during the July and August months my brother and I were at my grandmother's house in Montezuma. When I took the magazine home, my mother disapproved of my reading a movie magazine. I had to hide it under the mattress, which was where I also kept my secret diary.

Favorite childhood belongings:
    Candy cigarettes
    My leggins
    Fingernail polish
    Turquoise ring
    My doll, Gloria Lou
    My green ballerina dress
    My jacks and ball
    My blue velvet dress with the silver buttons

My roller skates
My blue mittens and my white mittens

Hated things:
Buster Brown shoes
My plaid school dresses

More favorites:
My silk hair ribbons
My barrettes
My Easter eggs

I LOVE A MYSTERY:
To be frightened with Jack, Doc and Reggie in their adventures while my brother and I did our homework was wonderful.

Lowell Thomas:
A voice, from the brown mahogany radio with gold lettering "Philco," announced events from the entire world. And he determined what kind of day the world had had. My father and his friends often talked about what Lowell Thomas said.

SNOW WHITE (the movie, age eight):
I thought after seeing this movie that somehow in some way we were all sleeping and had to be awakened before we could really live.

Pinocchio:
If you lied, something happened inside your body that made you change and people saw it. It didn't have to be a nose.

Judy Garland:
When she sang "Dear Mr. Gable," I knew someone else was full of yearning just like myself.

Marian Anderson, Eleanor Roosevelt, Mary Bethune, Helen Keller:
My father talked constantly of how great these women were, and urged me
to be like them.

Marian Anderson:
She was a model of behavior.

Mary Bethune:
She and Eleanor Roosevelt were models of worthy
deeds.

Billie Holiday:
She sang in a sad way I yearned to understand.

Kids who signed my autograph book:
It was a red book I bought at Kresge's with embossed flowers on the borders and sheets of pastel-colored paper. I carried it in my school bag. "To a Sweet Kid." "I'll never forget you." "To my best friend always." "To the greatest kid in the world."

My father (again):
He let me sing "Deep Purple" to him when he came home from work.

My mother:
My mother once bought long false braids to wear to a Halloween party. She dressed as a gypsy. After Halloween she put the long thick braids in her dresser drawer. When I didn't think anyone was looking, I'd take out the long braids and attach them to my hair and put on my mother's lipstick and her fingernail polish.

My grandmother:
She got up at dawn and worked tirelessly.

My grandfather:
He told me stories about people in the town, both white and Black.

Our minister, Rev. ———:
He was always angry when he finished preaching, and the congregation seemed angry. I was afraid of him. He had dark eyes and dressed in black robes. He seemed evil.

Snow White:
I often thought, why did Snow White's stepmother want her killed in the woods and to have her heart brought back in a box? To be the "fairest" in the kingdom must be very important.

My father (1937):

He took me to church with him Easter Sunday. I carried my small Easter basket and wore a round straw hat with cherries on the brim. It was wonderful to drive alone with my father in the car to the Lane Metropolitan Church. I was happy. We walked down the aisle into the church, a mammoth hall that had once been a Jewish temple.

White flowers covered the altar and members of the choir wore white as well. The minister preached violently of the crucifixion, Jesus, Judas, betrayal and finally Jesus Christ arising from the dead on Easter morning. My father started sobbing. (My father who smiled, laughed, made jokes, whistled, teased me.) I had never seen him cry.

Jesus had died a long time ago and he had *arisen* on Easter morning. Why was my father so very concerned about Jesus? I tried to hold his arm.

People in Montezuma and the English:
My mother often said that most of the white people of Montezuma's families came from England. I realized dimly that this meant some of our ancestors too had come from England, since, like most "Negro" families in the town, we had white relations as well as "Negro." I became very interested in "England."

Great-Aunt Mary Lee (a heroine to me):
Next door to her house she ran a one-room store that had a Coca-Cola sign on the front. Sometimes she'd let me wait on a customer. She told me about Aunt Ella.

My Great-Aunt Ella (who died before I was born):
She died as a young girl and I was "the spitting image of her," "looked just like her," Aunt Mary Lee and many of my father's relatives in Montezuma said of me. "Looks just like Ella," they'd say.

She was a little touched in the head, Aunt Mary told me once. "What's 'touched in the head'?" I asked.

"Oh," she said, "she used to sit up in the trees and sing. You're the spitting image of her."

Why, I wondered, did I have to look like someone dead who was "touched in the head"? Why didn't anyone say I looked like my mother, whom people even stared at and called "pretty"?

My cousins, the Brocks:
They lived on a farm outside of Montezuma, reached by long winding red roads, in a white house with a screen porch and a front garden of petunias and geraniums. Across the road from the house were acres of golden corn-fields. There was a barn, a carriage, a smokehouse, a weeping willow tree

with a swing and a long kitchen with a big stove. At five o'clock they all got up, and at six had a breakfast of biscuits, grits, fat meat and coffee or buttermilk. At one o'clock when my cousins came from the fields they had a dinner of several vegetables, chicken or ham and lemonade. We all sat at a long table with benches inside the screen porch that faced the backyard, the barn, the smokehouse and the peach trees.

On Sunday mornings my Uncle Otis hitched up the carriage so some of us could ride to church, which was down the road and in the woods. In the evening, after a supper of food left over from dinner, my cousins and I sat outside in the yard under the willow tree and told ghost stories.

Sometimes in the morning as soon as I awakened, I ran outside to swing in the weeping willow tree.

My favorite cousin was James. He was two years older than I was, had sandy hair, fair skin and blue-brown eyes. He liked to tease me. I loved him.

When he was in his twenties, he shot himself.

My Aunt Ruby:
She made dresses on Saturday afternoon for the girls to wear to church on Sunday morning. All Saturday evening she worked furiously on the sewing machine which sat in the living room, yards of colored cottons falling to the floor, miles of ribbons, buttons and threads piled on chairs. She would "stitch" a pretty dress in a few hours. While she stitched, we helped in the kitchen husking corn, snapping beans, picking chickens, making dough and cleaning up the house for Sunday.

Can't I live with you, I asked my Aunt Ruby. No, she laughed as she sat amid the mountains of beautiful cotton at the Singer sewing machine. "But I'll ask Ethel Lee"—my grandmother—"can you stay another week." How happy I was, another week with my sandy-haired cousins in their house amid the cornfields.

Mary Alice (my "distant" cousin):
She lived down the road from the Brocks with Aunt Hattie in a large faded white house that sat back, almost hidden from the road, amid willow trees. She and Hattie lived there alone in a house that seemed to have very little furniture and almost empty rooms with doors that were kept closed. At night Mary Alice ran amid the willow trees with a sheet pulled over her head. "I'm a ghost," she'd say.

23

Great-Uncle Marcus (the summer I was seven):
He was dying of tuberculosis and my great-aunt kept him in a room with a daybed, right off the kitchen. I never saw him stand or walk. But sometimes he'd cry out, "Come here, I want to talk to you." Sometimes I'd bring him a glass of water. Every morning my great-aunt made a huge breakfast for him and left it on the stove for a neighbor to give to him.

The next summer I went to Georgia the daybed was empty. I asked my great-aunt, where was Uncle Marcus? She didn't answer. Finally she said, "Why don't you go on out in the yard and play?"

Laurence Olivier:
My mother loved him.

England—Kings, Queens and THE SECRET GARDEN*:*
Of course I knew England was where Kings and Queens lived. And long before *Jane Eyre;* the heroine of *The Secret Garden*, my favorite book before *Jane Eyre*, she too had come from England. Mary was her name.

Queen Victoria, Chaucer, Shakespeare, William the Conqueror and Anne Boleyn:
They would all one day become characters in my plays.

Snow White:
After seeing the Disney movie, I'd think of Snow White in her casket in the woods. Why did Snow White have to die, even though her Prince's kiss would later awaken her? Why did she have to "sleep" in the casket in the woods?

People in the red autograph books:
I bought red autograph books at Kresge's, using them as diaries and writing about people in a coded language. I simply wrote backwards. I kept the red diaries under the mattress.

Frankenstein:
He killed people, yet he had a kind heart.

Dracula:
Even though he liked blood he was noble and even lived in a castle. Because of his nobility he could turn into a tiny bat and kill and make people grow fangs. He was Bela Lugosi.

Sherlock Holmes:
He was Basil Rathbone; he lived in a place called Baker Street in London.

Then there was *The Invisible Man, Jack the Ripper* and *The Woman in Black*.

Abe Lincoln:
Although he grew up in a log cabin, he became President and freed my forebears from slavery. Yet he had a mad wife.

Clissy:
She beat up little kids on the playground on summer mornings. Often this led to my sitting on the front steps hiding from her.

Explorers we read about:
Magellan, Marco Polo, Christopher Columbus. They traveled to unknown coasts, endured hardships, discovered.

Haile Selassie:
Photographs of him on his throne in Ethiopia with his leopards.

Person who wrote the song "My Ship Has Sails":

Miss Bell:

A fourth-grade teacher. She told my mother I would have a "nervous break-down" if I didn't stop trying to be the best in everything in class. My mother said I had to stop reading so much; I had to go outside and play. She made me sit on the front porch and refused to let me take my *Katy Did* books with me. I heard my mother tell my father what Miss Bell said as they disappeared into the kitchen. When my father came out of the kitchen he smiled at me and asked me would I like to go for a drive in the car (my favorite thing) and buy some ice cream. I could get Neapolitan (strawberry, chocolate, vanilla), my favorite kind. Naturally I didn't know what a nervous breakdown was.

Ginger Rogers and Fred Astaire (after seeing their movies):
Gracefulness must be sought. It's possible the sublime could exist in your daily life.

My mother:
Her china cabinets and hatboxes.
There is beauty in order.

An article (1930s) about my father:
It appeared in the *Cleveland Plain
Dealer* describing the intensity and
fruitfulness of his social work.
You're supposed to try to make an
imprint with your life.

Hitler:
He was the person who caused a
tower to be built in the school
playground across the street from our house, a frightening orange steel struc-
ture (a white light at its pinnacle shone at night into our windows) that was

surrounded by a jagged metal fence said to electrocute you if you touched it. This tower was a watchtower in case an attack from the Germans or the Japanese occurred.

Hitler caused my father to announce every evening from his armchair, as he read the evening *Cleveland Press*, the siege of ————, the killing of ————, the capture of ————, the bombing of ————, the worsening of the War and, in my mind, the possibility that from the tower the air raid warden would soon discover the enemy was marching into Ohio. Sometimes in the night I would awake and stand at the window in my pajamas and watch the tower, bright orange and hideous in the night. Would the Germans come in the back door? In *Mrs. Miniver* a German came into the rear of the house. Would they hide in the garage?

My Jewish friend Yvette told me that Hitler didn't like Jews and she and her widowed mother were afraid. Hitler didn't like anyone except the Aryan race . . . the blond race. When I went to see the movie *Hitler's Children*, with my brother and the kids from next door, we were very upset that Bonita Granville was beaten by the SS, the German officers in their strangely designed uniforms, helmets and boots. She was beaten with a whip because she didn't want to fight for Hitler. We were children. If Hitler came to Cleveland and we resisted, would we be beaten and sent to a concentration camp?

My mother said she was buying war bonds, and we gave up butter and meat, we saved coupons. I asked my father when he came home at night, was that helping? I didn't want the Nazis to come, I didn't want to be a Hitler's Child or go to a camp. My best friend said as long as the tower was up we were in danger.

The Japanese (age ten):
They bombed Pearl Harbor and because of them Roosevelt declared War and my mother no longer was at home at lunchtime because she went to work at a War plant (Fisher Body). I had to make peanut butter sandwiches for myself and my brother and take care of him from twelve to one-fifteen when school started again. It was because of the Japanese that my mother sprained her back at the War plant. She had to stay in bed for days. And she limped. I was afraid.

My grandfather:
He was rich. He owned acres and acres of peach orchards in Georgia. My mother said he employed a lot of people. He had a chauffeur who wore a black uniform and hat and he lived in a sprawling, charming house with a sunporch and a garden. I concluded it was desirable to own peach orchards.

Jack Benny:
He provided our family with its happiest times. We all sat around the Philco radio on Sunday night, eating Neapolitan ice cream with its three flavors, and laughed at Jack, Rochester, Mary, Phil, Dennis and Carmichael, Jack Benny's bear.

Stella Dallas:
My mother told me she felt similar to this soap heroine. She "liked her." Stella Dallas had many problems which made my mother look sad. I wondered why. And as she cooked the dinner after we had turned off the radio I watched my mother, wondering why.

Man in the Moon:
Wonder.

Bogie Man and the Devil
  (as a child):
They were waiting and at their whim might attack you, even kill you.

Cleveland Indians (baseball team):
Our heroes.

Arenzia, Doris and Mildred:
The kids next door—my cohorts in I Spy, Hopscotch, Hide and Seek, Marbles, and Jacks, and on swings and parallel bars. Pure delights of childhood.

My mother:
Who made jello, fried chicken, strawberry shortcake and cakes with vanilla icing and lemonade and tuna fish sandwiches.

My great-aunt (in Georgia):
Who churned home-made vanilla ice cream on Sunday.

My grandmother (in Georgia):
She made biscuits and fried fish for breakfast followed by a dipper full of mineral water from the well at the foot of the road.

Lorenzo Jones, Backstage Wife:
Hero and heroine of radio soap operas.

The announcer of LET'S PRETEND:
A fanciful Saturday-morning children's radio story.

Mr. Bertiloni:
My next-door neighbor who built a beautiful tiny grape arbor in his front yard. Twice he let his niece, Angie, and me sit inside the arbor on a bench. We ate purple grapes. Angie told me her uncle had had a grape arbor in Italy before he came to "this country."

Wolf Man (Lon Chaney):
Although I slept soundly at night, I felt there must be a truth to tales of the moon and changing. My mother often complained of being unable to sleep, lying "awake all night," and the following morning "not being herself." Sometimes she had dark circles under her eyes.

People in my mother's dreams:
People whom my mother saw at night had often "been dead for years." I didn't know anyone who had been dead for years. So her dreams held a spectacular fascination. "My Aunt Hattie," "my stepfather," "my grandmother," "my mother," all were people who had been dead a long time. But from my mother's dreams, I got to know them. They all were from Georgia. They were all from the town my parents were born in, Montezuma.

Anonymous people (who wrote the songs we sang at camp, around the campfire, in the dining hall and in the chapel in the woods):
> "Let Me Call You Sweetheart"
> "My Darling Clementine"
> "And the Green Grass Grows All Around"
> "Keep the Lamp Light Burning"
> "Fight the Team Across the Field, Show Them Ohio's Here, Keep the Earth Reverberating with a Mighty Cheer, Rah-rah-rah"
> and "God Bless America"

People in LIFE, LOOK, PARENTS *and* GOOD HOUSEKEEPING:
In the summer my mother let me open the *Good Housekeeping* to a page of a perfect-looking, extravagant cake or pie, then left the kitchen after setting everything needed on the table for the creation. Halfway through I usually gave up on my cake and the *Good Housekeeping* cake resembling each other, and settled for often disheveled-looking cake or pie. My brother *always* said it was *good*.

Charles Dickens (A CHRISTMAS CAROL, the version we read in elementary school, abridged):
Ebenezer Scrooge lived out different periods of his entire life in one night, a concept that was so appealing that it would haunt me twenty years later in my own writing, a concept I would work very hard at capturing, living through epochs of your life within an hour or an evening or a night.

The Zingales:
My friend's family spoke Italian at home to each other. One of the beginnings of my love of that beautiful language.

Mr. Bertiloni and his wife:
They spoke Italian to each other as they quietly worked in the grape arbor in their front yard. I peered through the hedge and listened to them.

Barnum & Bailey Circus:
They came to Cleveland every spring. How thrilling to sit in the three-ring circus with all the children from the Cleveland public schools watching lions,

bears, trapeze artists and clowns while we ate Cracker Jacks and cotton candy and listened to the circus music.

Animal Crackers:
I hated to eat them—but then there were always other boxes on the shelf at the corner grocery store. But eating the little "animals" could sometimes give me pause.

Dick and Jane and their parents and their dog, Spot:
Our family was like theirs (I would think proudly) except we didn't have a dog. That is undoubtedly the reason I often pestered my mother to buy us a little dog. Then our family could be more like this model family that our class read about during all of our early elementary school days.

Charlie McCarthy (Edgar Bergen's Charlie):
He was impertinent to adults and even made fun of them, something I secretly longed to do even as I remained the epitome of the sweet, quiet child. "How well behaved she is," everyone said.

Rita Hayworth:
If a person had red hair and could dance, the world belonged to her.

Anne of Green Gables:
Another heroine with "red hair." "Carrot-colored" hair seemed to present a person with a wonderful destiny.

My father:
In the evening when he came in from work, my father sat me on his knee in the dark maroon armchair and read me Paul Lawrence Dunbar, sometimes "Little Brown Baby wif Spa'klin' Eyes."

Kate Smith (on the radio) singing "God Bless America":
My elementary school class (Italian, Jewish, Negro, Irish, Polish) every morning sang "My Country 'Tis of Thee" and then we put our hands to our foreheads, stood facing the flag and said, "I pledge allegiance to the flag of the United States of America and to the republic for which it stands." Every morning for six years.

My mother:

She would sometimes disappear to the hallway steps outside the kitchen and close the door behind her. I could hear her crying. When she came back into the kitchen, she wouldn't speak but would dry the dishes or peel potatoes for dinner. I could not imagine why she cried.

People my mother dreamed about:

In the morning I could hardly wait to hear about them. The stories she told of them were as exciting as the movies of Frankenstein and Dracula that I saw at the Waldorf.

These people my mother dreamed about continued to grow in my imagination. Like the people in the red scrapbook, they often knew each other and had known my parents when they were young.

I would list them in my mind as I sat on the front steps of our house (the steps that faced the orange tower).

Her mother who died when she was three.

Her stepfather who was killed walking across an electrified railroad track.

Her Aunt Hattie who died when my mother was pregnant with me.

When my mother was making oatmeal on winter mornings as I sat waiting with my bowl at the kitchen table, I secretly yearned that my mother would talk *more* about people she had dreamed about. There is no doubt that a person talking about the people in his or her dreams became an archetype for people in my monologues, plays and stories.

Clark Gable:

Although I loved my grandparents immensely, I hated the train ride to Georgia that my brother and I took every June, especially the ride from Cincinnati to Montezuma in the dirty Jim Crow car. When the Traveler's Aid met us in the Cincinnati station, my brother was still crying. He was about seven then, and as soon as the train pulled out of the Cleveland Terminal Tower he started to cry and he cried all the way to Cincinnati. Night would come while we rode into the South and he cried with his head on my shoulder. My father had bought me some magazines at the Cleveland Terminal. One was a *Modern Screen* with a picture of Clark Gable in an army uniform.

I tried to interest my brother in the magazine, but he kept sobbing, "I want to go home." I put my arm around my brother, looked out of the dirty double-panel windows and clutched the *Modern Screen* magazine with Gable on the cover.

My grandmother and church:
When I walked up the road with my grandmother to the white wooden church, I felt we were in a holy procession like the people on the Sunday school cards . . . the golden red road, the blue sky, the neighbors walking ahead of us. One day I would see a book of Giotto prints and think of these processions on the road. And use his colors in my stories, not realizing how I had connected the Sunday school card colors, the Georgia landscape colors and colors of Giotto.

My grandmother, our twinship and the Montezuma English:
Besides Aunt Ella, people said I looked like my grandmother when she was a girl. In my great-aunt's parlor, among the pictures on the wall was a large photograph of my grandmother in a long pale dress at about age nine. All of my grandmother's friends said I looked exactly like that picture. At least the ones who didn't say I looked like Aunt Ella. But this picture of my grandmother at age nine was the source of many conversations, especially since I was about that age. I began, over the successive summers, to feel that picture was my image.

   Now I wear jackets over dresses just as my grandmother wore jackets over her dresses. And I have always tried to arrange my furniture to look like her front parlor. She and my great-aunt were both servants in the same household, a family that owned a canning factory and lived in a house that, to my mind, looked like pictures of Monticello. That accounted for the fact that their (my grandmother's and great-aunt's) closets were filled with hatboxes from Saks Fifth Avenue and they both wore dresses from Atlanta. Most of the things they both owned had once belonged to the M—— family, who were of English descent.

   When I visited the M—— house with my grandmother, it was clear their rooms looked like the rooms in the movie *David Copperfield*. And other movies about England that we had seen at the Waldorf.

Sarah Clara:

When my grandmother went to work every morning, my brother and I walked down the road to Aunt Mary Lee's house, but if Aunt Mary Lee was working (they were servants in the same wealthy household) then my grandmother would leave us at Sarah Clara's house, a few doors away.

Sarah Clara, my grandmother always said, was the prettiest girl in Montezuma. She and her grandparents lived in a yellow-and-white frame house with giant sunflowers in the front yard. Sarah Clara was sixteen and told me stories of high school. Her boyfriend gave her a bottle of Tabu cologne and she let me smell the Tabu and even put a drop on my cheek, and she let me see her long yellow dotted Swiss evening dress that she had worn to the high school dance.

Many summer afternoons my brother and I sat on Sarah Clara's porch until my grandmother came home. I daydreamed of a day when I would have a bottle of Tabu and a long yellow evening dress and go to high school. Sarah Clara! One day she even put on her long yellow dress and walked around the porch. How could I know that years later, one summer sitting in a house on Piazza Donatello in Florence, I would create two heroines, and one's name would be Sarah and the other, heroine in a play called *The Owl Answers*, would be named Clara.

My great-aunt and my grandmother, their landscape:

Their houses, surrounded by petunias, hedges, sunflowers, magnolia trees, their wells, their blue-and-white dishes, the dippers and bucket, their pot-bellied stoves, the porches with wicker furniture, the smell of wood burning in the stoves, the way the houses sat on the Georgia roads . . . the picket fences . . . these houses with their vistas of cornfields, vegetable gardens, fig trees, flower gardens that faced the road, the porch that wound around the house, the stone paths that led to the steps . . . these houses were the most beautiful houses in the world to me.

My great-aunt:
It was next to her house that the one-room store with the Coca-Cola sign on the front sat. She ran the store when she wasn't working in the M——— household. My mother said people said Aunt Mary Lee had "a pretty penny although she was close-mouthed about it."

It was impossible for me to see that this Georgia landscape became in my mind what "landscape" was.

My mother and Jane Eyre:
My mother often told me that she had been sent away to boarding school at the age of five and remained there until she was seventeen. Her mother was dead and her father thought boarding school was the best course for her. On holidays, she said, she would get very lonely and the headmaster of the school (in Fort Valley, Georgia) would invite her to his house. I thought my mother's childhood life very strange. Everyone I knew went to a public school and I had never ever seen a boarding school, that "one" was sent away to. It was very difficult for me to imagine even though my mother spoke of it often. Finally when I was eleven I took a book out of the school library that was gray with green designs—a pretty book, I thought—and it was called *Jane Eyre*.

Almost before the first chapter was concluded, it was decided that the heroine, Jane Eyre, would be "sent away to boarding school." How excited I was as I sat in the small rocking chair in my room. Here was a little girl who had a life like my mother's. It was so thrilling that I read the first section about Jane Eyre at Lowood many times. I began to envy my mother's exotic upbringing. It wasn't fair that I would go every day to Lafayette Public School when she had lived a life like Jane Eyre's.

As much as it was possible I used to imagine that I had been my mother when she was a little girl. I think after *Jane Eyre*, when she told me stories, I almost believed they had happened to me: her life at boarding school, her pictures in the red scrapbook of herself in white organdy dresses standing by a Model T Ford, the people in her dreams and maybe most of all her incredibly pretty hair that everyone commented on. I think now that I often thought they were mine. They all belonged to me.

Years later my obsession with hair would again and again reveal itself in my work.

Mary in THE SECRET GARDEN:

She too, like Jane Eyre, was "sent away," as my mother had been "sent away." How wonderful my mother was that she so resembled people in books. My life seemed drab next to her life. When I grew up I had to do "something" . . . "something" like the people in these books.

I wanted to be in books too.

JUNIOR HIGH
1943 – 1946

Miss Eichenbaum and Chopin
Writing to the movie stars
Hearing of "artistic struggle"

Junior high, myself (1943):
My father often called me good-looking when in the mirror I saw a strange-looking face.

I kept stacks of *Modern Screen* in the vanity table drawer and made a scrapbook from my favorite pictures. I especially liked pictures of people at parties in evening dress. And I kept another scrapbook on Ingrid Bergman. How marvelous to have a Swedish accent and a radiant smile.

Sometimes when no one was home, I'd go to the attic and get my mother's old blue-and-white dotted Swiss evening gown and try it on and sit at my vanity table with my movie photos lined up in the mirror and daydream of being at the Brown Derby.

Myself:
I thought I looked funny in my plaid skirts and white blouses with my straightened hair curled in tiny curls.

Roosevelt and Churchill:
They were meeting. I saw it in the newsreel at the Waldorf Theatre. They were meeting to stop the War, they were sitting in chairs smiling, Churchill had a cigar and President Roosevelt smoked a cigarette with a long holder. They were here, there, they were in Malta. How, I wondered, could they,

sitting in chairs smiling, stop the Germans? My father had told me that the Germans were invading *all* of Europe. I was very worried; then my father told me the Russians were going to help. The Russians were going to help us.

The Russians (the Russian Bear):
My father was smiling, the newspaper under his arm as he strode into the house. The Russian Bear is stopping Hitler. Then Paris was liberated. We wouldn't have to use coupons to buy butter or meat. We wouldn't have to wonder whether we were eating horsemeat. And most of all, I wouldn't have to worry about being taken from my parents to be a Hitler's Child. We could go peacefully back to roller skating on the sidewalk and reading comics on the front porch. Soon they would take the tower down.

Miss Eichenbaum (my piano teacher):
Her family had fled from Warsaw. We had to go up the stairs to the room where she taught piano. She wore a large beige cardigan sweater over dark dresses. She gave me a tiny bust of Chopin and one of Schumann. She was the first person to talk of "artistic struggle." The top of her piano was filled with photographs of her family and statues of Mozart, Beethoven and Chopin. At the end of each year, at the time of the recital, she gave me another bust of a composer. It was because of Miss Eichenbaum that I went to see the movie *A Song to Remember*, the story of Chopin's life.

Esther Clements:
My seventh-grade music teacher made us learn portions of *Tannhäuser*. She spoke of "power" and "rebelliousness" in music, words that burned in my twelve-year-old mind.

Miss Edwards:
My eighth-grade English teacher taught Shelley, Keats, Byron, Wordsworth. The words "poetic," "lyrical," "romantic" suggested that writers led meaningful, significant lives and as they expressed sorrow and great happiness they were still often misfits, at odds with society. Thoughts a thirteen-year-old "Negro" girl responded to.

Chopin:
After Miss Eichenbaum told me of Chopin, even though I was not advanced enough to play the pieces, I bought a book of polonaises and "struggled" with sections of them. It was then I understood that *if* I had the technique and the experience I would be able to capture this beauty on the piano. (As they were played in the movie; that was my lesson.)

Junior high:
In the evenings after I'd done my homework I'd sit at the kitchen table and write penny postcards to the movie stars to get their autographed photos. Toby, who sat in front of me in seventh-grade homeroom, gave me her list of the movie studios

> MGM
> Universal
> Twentieth Century–Fox
> Warner Brothers
> David O. Selznick

that she had carefully copied on notebook paper. I carried the list in my school bag at all times with my fingernail polish, cologne and natural-color Tangee lipstick that I was allowed to have but not yet wear.

Frank Sinatra:
On the Saturday-night *Hit Parade.*

Orson Welles (in the movie of
   JANE EYRE):
He was Edward Rochester, whom Jane Eyre loved; therefore I loved him.

My classmates at Empire Junior High:
Like the kids at Lafayette, they had parents who had been born in Europe; but in our new neighbor-

hood (Glenville) it was not Italy . . . but Poland, Czechoslovakia, Hungary and Russia.

Orson Welles:
I wrote a penny postcard to him at one of the movie studios.

> Dear Mr. Welles:
>
> I liked you in *Jane Eyre*. Please send me an autographed photo.

It arrived one lovely June day in a white envelope, a large 5×7 picture (not the usual 2×3 size of the other photos, especially those from MGM). It was signed, in remarkably authentic-looking ink, "Orson Welles." I convinced myself it was original. Before I could mount the photo in my scrapbook, my brother got peanut butter on it. I screamed at him and started to cry. He looked amazed and walked away.

Lana Turner:
I kept reading that she was "discovered" in a drugstore. Being "discovered" seemed to be something necessary for happiness. Would I ever be "discovered," and what could I do to even be considered? It really worried me.

My best friend's Aunt Nina:
She wore huge, wide-brimmed hats, voile dresses and fox furs. She painted the interior of their house rose and white, then put prints of French Impressionists on the wall. Her family had dinner in a formal style—with a linen tablecloth and a maid to serve them. I found that spellbinding. She struck me as having great imagination which she lived by. She was romantic.

M. Susko (my locker partner in junior high):
She told me she had nothing to look forward to in life because at sixteen she *had* to quit school and help her father in his funeral business, which she did.

T. Sabin (my junior high gym leader-partner):
She was the first person my age whom I ever heard describe her parents as if they were people. She'd say: My father has had to work hard all his life. And since he was very young he's been a merchant marine. But he has a small view of life and people and expects me to live my life as he wants me

to. He keeps my mother shut up in the house and won't let her go anywhere or work. He expects us to wait on him when he's home and he's mean. I'm going to lead a different life. I'm not going to be like my mother. (For a start she was the second-highest student in our high school class, five years later.)

Freddy Jamison:
I was still secretly in love with him, but my mother didn't approve of him. I wrote about him in the autograph books I hid under the mattress.

Miss McCreary:
I did well in our journalism class and informed Miss McCreary, our teacher, that I wanted to be a journalist. She said she didn't think, because of my color, that it was realistic for me to pursue that thought.

Louis Jordan, Nat King Cole, Billy Eckstine, Frank Sinatra:
Said romance and joy awaited me.

Elizabeth Taylor (in JANE EYRE):
She was Jane Eyre's best friend, Helen, and as a child died of pneumonia because cruel Mr. Brocklehurst punished her and made her walk in the rain after he had cut off her hair.

My mother and her hair:
When my mother cut her hair I used to beg her to let me keep the strands.

KING'S ROW:
I heard my mother's friends talk about *King's Row*. My mother had a copy of the popular novel down in the nightstand in her room. I "stole" it and read it.

People in the novel and movie KING'S ROW (popular in the early '40s):
I sensed that under the surface of the adult world lay betrayals, hatred, infidelities. *King's Row* became the map which I, at thirteen, used to interpret my own adult community which adolescence was bringing me into.

People in MODERN SCREEN *magazine:*
They wore evening dress and jewels and sat at small round tables in places called Ciro's, the Coconut Grove, the Brown Derby, while photographers photographed their magical lives. I yearned to be like that. And I went upstairs and tried to comb my hair like Kathryn Grayson's in a pompadour and for at least a day tried to perfect a Swedish Ingrid Bergman accent like the one she had in *Gaslight*. I ordered photos every week from the movie studios which I carefully put in scrapbooks, meticulously gluing every corner. One scrapbook had black paper and every star's name was written under the photograph in white ink. No one was allowed to touch it.

People:
Those I saw walking in the snow on my street one Christmas afternoon.

My friends in the Saturday Social at Seven:
My parents and their friends formed a club for their children who were twelve to fifteen. We met once a month at the Y and learned to dance. How I dreaded it. But we did get to listen to Nat King Cole, Billy Eckstine and Louis Jordan and His Typany Five.

Nat King Cole:
He sang the songs we fell in love to:

> "My Lips Remember Your Kisses"
> "Christmas Song"
> "Nature Boy"

> We went to see him at the Palace. He had a white piano.

Billy Eckstine:
He sang "In My Solitude." We were in love with him.

Frank Sinatra:
He was on *Hit Parade* and sang "Moonlight Becomes You." He sang at a place called the Paramount in New York and people fainted.

Paul Henreid and Bette Davis and Now, Voyager:
The idea of going on an ocean journey and becoming transformed by it caught fire in my mind when I saw *Now, Voyager*. Not only did this seem to happen to Bette Davis in *Now, Voyager*, but long journeys seemed to be a part of the destiny of people in many of the books I loved. Mary in *The Secret Garden*, *Heidi* and, again, *Jane Eyre*.

Bette Davis:
The heroines in her movies were reflective and independent and had opinions. They also dressed beautifully and were adored by men. I wanted to be like that.

Ingrid Bergman:
She was worshipped in her movies and always spoke honestly about her feelings.

Marguerite C. (our neighbor):
She painted her nails the same color as the shade of her lipstick and collected *Vogue* magazines from the 1930s. Her entire attic was piled high with issues of *Vogue* and *Look*. She bought clothes in the style of the Duchess of Windsor and prided herself on reading every Book-of-the-Month Club selection. She had been one of the first "Negro" women (in the 1920s) to get a degree from Cleveland's prestigious Western Reserve University.

My parents' friends:
I envied them. To me they possessed a glamour. They drank highballs and smoked cigarettes, read *Crisis* magazine and the *Pittsburgh Courier* . . . were members of the NAACP and the Urban League, were members of the Alphas, Kappas, the AKAs, the Deltas and Sigmas, played bridge, poker, tonk. They formed social clubs whose doings were reported in the *Cleveland Call and Post*. They loved formal dances (especially at holidays), Lena, Duke, Cab; worshipped A. Philip Randolph, Paul Robeson, W. E. B. Du Bois, Marian Anderson, Joe Louis, Sugar Ray Robinson and Mary Bethune.

They worked a lifetime at their jobs as teachers, social workers, civic workers, doctors and lawyers. They shopped at May Company, Higbee's

and Halle's. They bought their first houses during World War II, often with the family's—that is, the wife's—"second income." They organized social clubs for their children, pushed them to do well in school, encouraged them to enter professions. They were devoted to the "Negro Cause." They worked hard, very hard, to maintain all of this.

MILDRED PIERCE, *Mildred Pierce's daughter, Ann Blyth:*
Everybody said I was "so sweet." Sometimes I longed to be bad like Mildred Pierce's daughter.

LEAVE HER TO HEAVEN, *Gene Tierney:*
When Gene Tierney drowned her husband's young brother in the middle of a lake, I had no idea that sixteen years later I would find expression for the despair of one of my characters by using the same image, drowning in a lake. And it would be a main character based on myself.

THE SEVENTH VEIL, *Ann Todd:*
This movie that said the heroine, Ann Todd, wore "veils" to mask her hidden thoughts, feelings and personae fascinated me. Later when I wrote, I tried to articulate this concept but failed. Not until I visited West Africa in 1960 and was surrounded by African masks did I see how I could use the "veiled" concept. I simply had my character hide behind an African mask.

THE CONSTANT NYMPH, *Tessa:*
Charles Boyer loved Tessa, the young heroine of this movie, so for a summer I secretly called myself Tessa.

Philippa Schuyler:
My mother's friends were all talking of her . . . how she looked, where she had traveled and how she would soon be appearing in Cleveland, playing the piano.

I played the piano too, having bought piles of sheet music from Kresge's . . . music far too advanced for me. And after school I tried to play these advanced pieces of Schumann and Chopin, refusing to hear Miss Eichenbaum's words that I wasn't ready. I thought if I practiced maybe one day my mother's friends would talk of me and I would "appear" and "travel." After all, I had been taking piano lessons since I was eight.

Philippa Schuyler:
My parents took me to see her, she was my age, my skin color . . . she made a deep impression. She was written of, talked of. She astounded. I realized after I saw her that I would never be able to really play the piano. I begged my mother to let me *stop* taking piano lessons. I put away all my music books and shut the piano.

"What happened?" my mother said. "You used to love it so." But I knew, not only had I not been really good in the recitals, but now it was clear I could never be a Philippa Schuyler, a prodigy. I kept my thoughts to myself and told my mother I didn't have time to practice.

"I don't understand," she said.

Favorite high school things:
Tortoiseshell chest with a bottle of cologne inside. A bottle of Prince Match-

abelli cologne with its golden crown top, peach chiffon evening dress, a present of yellow roses for my first formal dance.

Dr. Sam Sheppard:
Now that the war was over, violence never crossed my mind until the murder of Marilyn Sheppard. The idea that a pregnant woman could be murdered in her room on the shores of Lake Erie seemed only possible in the novel *King's Row* or *Leave Her to Heaven*. I reread both books many times. I had never known anyone who had murdered or who was murdered. We talked of it all summer. Its national notoriety changed our lives. Was the bushy-haired murderer still hiding on the nearby shores of Lake Erie or was Dr. Sheppard a killer? It filled the pages of our newspapers, the *Plain Dealer*, the *Press*. We talked of it past summer into the icy winter.

My mother, Lena Horne and myself as a grown-up:
My mother looked to me to be a combination of Lena Horne and Ingrid Bergman. I thought she was the prettiest person I'd ever seen. But I couldn't

look forward to growing up and looking like her . . . everyone said we looked nothing alike. I was often unhappy about this fact that when I grew up (no matter what else happened to me) I would never look like this beautiful woman with brown curly hair, pale luminous skin and keen elegant features.

My mother and my face:
My face as an adult will always seem to be lacking because it is not my mother's face.

HIGH SCHOOL
1 9 4 6 – 1 9 4 9

My friends and teachers
My grandmother's death
Julius Caesar
JANE EYRE, *continued*
THE GLASS MENAGERIE

Myself:
I begged my mother to buy me a cashmere sweater. Marlene Katz had twelve (more than any girl in our school—she even had three cashmere sweater sets). My mother finally agreed to buy one. It was yellow.

Elsie Jacobs wore angora sweaters and socks that matched in addition to having almost as many cashmeres as Marlene. They both enjoyed great status in our homeroom, especially since they were also "brains."

My friends (Rachel, Norma, Barbara):
We went on double dates: to the movies, horseback riding at an old farm outside of Cleveland and rowing in Rockefeller Park, where we also played tennis and bicycled down Snake Hill. We went to football games and track meets and lived for Friday-night Y dances after spending the week planning how we would dress exactly alike.

My friends:
At least in high school, on weekends we got to wear taffeta cocktail dresses with boat necklines, dresses trimmed in net or lace, dresses of silk shantung, moiré, pale wool and peau de soie. We got to wear pearl earrings, hats with little veils, lipsticks, powders and colognes.

Even my everyday skirts and sweaters began to seem more elegant, and I'd learned to comb my hair so that it wasn't a mass of little straightened curls.

I'd learned to make a pageboy.

Myself:

I forgot about being in books. And I had no plan to read straight through the school library as I had in elementary school and junior high school.

Wordsworth:

Wordsworth was often on my mind . . . the reflective quality of "Lines Composed a Few Miles Above Tintern Abbey."

> Five years have passed; five summers, with the length
> Of five long winters! and again I hear
> These waters, rolling from their mountain-springs
> With a soft inland murmur.—Once again
> Do I behold these steep and lofty cliffs,
> Which on a wild secluded scene impress
> Thoughts of more deep seclusion; and connect

The landscape with the quiet of the sky. . . .
These beauteous forms,
Through a long absence, have not been to me
As is a landscape to a blind man's eye:
But oft, in lonely rooms, and 'mid the din
Of towns and cities, I have owed to them . . .

I thought in my way I would like to speak of recollections while sitting in rooms—and soon rooms, the rooms of my characters, would find their way into my work with force.

Wordsworth and my father:
Was Wordsworth not unlike my father, saying often "When I was a boy"? And then he'd talk about "Papa," "Mama," "My Aunt Mary Lee." "When I was a boy," he'd say, "Mama, Papa, Mama, Papa . . ." He had been the only child and the center of their life and they his. . . . Years later on his deathbed, he said to me, "Mama, Papa, Mama, Papa, I'll see them soon."

But then he had said, "Mama, Papa, I remember." When I went to Georgia as a child, I slept in his boyhood room. The window faced a small cornfield. The room was exactly as it had been when my father was a boy. My grandmother's imagination imbued all her rooms with charm. This room had a large brass bed, a marble nightstand with a blue-and-white pitcher and basin to wash in, a mahogany dresser with a large mirror, a hooked rug beside the bed.

Percy Shelley and my grandmother:
In the summer of 1943 we had moved into a new house in the popular Glenville section of Cleveland, far across the city from the Mount Pleasant area with Mr. Bertiloni's grape arbor. These houses were larger. My parents even had a room with a fireplace, a room that ran the length of the house. It's a

Now, Voyager room, I used to think when I'd enter and my mother would be sitting in her pink quilted bedjacket reading *Cosmopolitan* and eating Whitman's chocolates (evenings, after she had completed her school work). By now she was teaching elementary school and was also completing her bachelor's degree and had college classes at night.

In the new house there was a bookcase in the living room next to the fireplace and on the bottom shelf were some old books left by the previous tenants. One book was crimson, the same crimson color as my mother's scrapbook, a thick volume with heavy pages entitled:

THE POEMS OF PERCY SHELLEY.

Sometimes after I'd finished my seventh-grade homework, I'd sit on the floor beside the bookcase and stare at the pretty old scarlet volume, and leaf through its thick pages. Eventually one poem, a brief one, caught my eye. I read it many times.

> Music, when soft voices die,
> Vibrates in the memory;
> Odors, when sweet violets sicken,
> Live within the sense they quicken.
> Rose leaves, when the rose is dead,
> Are heaped on the beloved's bed;
> And so thy thoughts, when thou art gone,
> Love itself shall slumber on.

The volume of Shelley remained on the bottom shelf of the bookcase behind the glass doors through the next years, during which my ninth-grade teacher, Miss Edwards, would speak to our class of Percy Shelley, his "lyricism," "the beauty of his language," his "wanderings." The volume remained there until the Christmas when I was fifteen and my grandmother died. She died days before Christmas. On Christmas our house was sad. We had returned from her funeral in Georgia, where my father had thrown himself upon her flower-heaped coffin and sobbed. That Christmas Day he hadn't come downstairs. It was early evening. There was a heaviness in the house. I sat down by the bookcase, took out the crimson Shelley volume and read:

Music, when soft voices die,
Vibrates in the memory;
Odors, when sweet violets sicken,
Live within the sense they quicken.

My grandmother and my father's room:

When my grandmother died, I remembered how amazing and wonderful it had been to stay in my father's room at her house every summer. Then when I had awakened each summer morning, I was looking out of the same window, onto the cornfield that my father had looked at when he had awakened. In the front room were pictures of my father as a boy standing in front of this very house. The manner in which my grandmother arranged pictures made looking at them as exciting as going to the Waldorf on a Saturday afternoon.

My father's room and my grandmother's front room with its leather settees and Victrola and the parlor at my great-aunt's house that my brother and I were allowed in only one hour on Sunday—it was a room of settees, ferns, china cabinets and photographs of all of the five sisters—are without a doubt the most influential and powerful rooms of my life.

It is still why I try to grow ferns that do not live; why I arrange every apartment with a clustering of photos. And why, finally, after years of searching . . . for their environment . . . my characters live in powerful, influential rooms, almost to the exclusion of the outside world.

THE GLASS MENAGERIE:

I saw the play and for the first time understood there were other family secrets, family joys and sorrows, just as in my own family.

Rachel:
My best friend and neighbor played the first violin in our high school orchestra. She explained how greatly a conductor could influence the orchestra, an idea that seemed amazing to me.

Bob Hope:
He had gone briefly to my junior high school, Empire, and that gave me a sense that a person from my junior high school could become known to the whole world. How remarkable that seemed.

OUR TOWN (Thornton Wilder):
We read the play. The passions of the average person have glory and importance, and what I felt as I walked to school each morning along the streets with maple trees might even be significant. After all, Emily was my age and she lived in a "town" not unlike Cleveland. Was what our family did important enough to write about? To read about?

THE BARRETTS OF WIMPOLE STREET (a high school production):
Poets are often sickly people and lead very romantic lives.

Edgar Allan Poe:
"Annabel Lee," which I memorized for a tenth-grade English class presentation:

> It was many and many a year ago,
> In a kingdom by the sea . . .

People:
Whom I'd see walking on the shores of Lake Erie in the summer near my house.

Larry Doby:
The Cleveland Indians baseball player lived on our street. A celebrity is a person who even sometimes in the early afternoon walks to the store to get the newspaper.

Tennessee Williams:
After we saw *The Glass Menagerie* with Julie Haydon, after Tom came to the edge of the stage and spoke his monologue and told Laura to "blow out her candles," I didn't understand for a long time that it was that summer evening when the idea of being a writer and seeing my own family onstage caught fire in my mind. But I wrote no play for years.

Myself:
Although by now it was expected of me to become a teacher like my mother or a social worker like my father, I secretly wrote stories and sent them to *Seventeen* magazine. And I, of course, continued my secret thoughts in notebooks I hid under the mattress.

Mr. Tucker:
Our high school Glee Club teacher, he had gone to Juilliard and he taught us one spring all the lovely songs of Rodgers and Hart. Even now when I walk on the Upper West Side where I have lived for years I find myself humming "Manhattan": "We'll go to Coney and eat baloney on a roll. In Central Park we'll stroll."

HAMLET:
We read *Hamlet* in the twelfth grade. Hamlet was torn between his parents.

Hester in THE SCARLET LETTER:
Severe inescapable punishment lies ahead for a woman who commits a sin.

Lena Horne:
I'd seen her on the stage at the Palace Theatre at age eleven—a Negro woman, a beautiful, vital spectacle.

In the MGM movies as a "Negro" woman, she was magical, romantic, a person of hypnotic glamour.

My mother's friends (mostly elementary school teachers):
They wore print dresses, hats and gloves and talked about their husbands and their children, their jobs, their students, while they played bridge.

Rodin, Shakespeare, Goethe:
Their statues in nearby Rockefeller Park with gardens named after them said that if you create, a beautiful garden may one day be named in your memory.

Chekhov, Joan and her mother:
I was invited to visit Joan and her widowed mother on a summer Sunday afternoon. When I arrived they sat very still in the living room of the small house reading *The Cherry Orchard* aloud to each other. My friend and her mother sitting together reading aloud a play by someone called Chekhov enchanted me. "He's a great Russian writer," Joan told me. Over our lunch she and her mother told me the story of *The Cherry Orchard.*

Joan's father (a lawyer) had died the year before, and when she came to study hall, where she sat in front of me, she had written me notes telling me how sad their house was now and how her mother (who had never worked) had to get a job as a salesclerk.

But now on this pretty afternoon as they talked of Chekhov they were joyful. On Sunday afternoons after church and before dinner in our family we listened to the baseball game or *Ted Mack's Amateur Hour* or sometimes André Kostelanetz. But we had never sat and read a play aloud. And it was Joan, one of the most-loved girls in our class (some say the most), who suggested we all go see a play called *The Glass Menagerie.*

Leonard:
He was the editor of our high school paper and told me that the high school editor "must" rebel against the teachers and our principal; that our paper had to tell the *truth* about things.

Mr. Davis and Jane Eyre:
In our drama class we read *Our Town, Night Must Fall, The Petrified Forest* and *Street Scene.* Mr. Davis told us about his summer and holiday trips to New York, where he saw Broadway plays. In the final project we had to do

a ten-minute characterization from a play. I asked him if I could do a monologue from *Jane Eyre* (the novel).

I wore a maroon-colored velvet jumper and a white ruffled blouse, trying to dress up like Joan Fontaine in the movie. I read the passage over and over and memorized it (the moment when Jane leaves Rochester). It was the only time in my life I publicly had a chance to become Jane Eyre. Even I could feel the passion I evoked in the class.

You have imagination, Mr. Davis said.

All the people who sang "race songs":
We heard them on jukeboxes in Negro restaurants. The passion.

JET, EBONY *magazines:*
A Negro could build a publishing empire.

Marie Curie:
Her daughter's book portrayed Madame Curie and her husband, Pierre Curie, working feverishly together in a shed, being challenged, thinking and rethinking scientific problems, being illuminated, isolating factors, rejecting equations, exhausted. Yet pursuing, discovering. What a perfect life, I thought.

My high school friends:
Some of them were going to Israel to live when they graduated. They were going to live on a "kibbutz."

One boy came to Glenville who had been in a concentration camp. He marched in a goosestep like a Nazi and did not speak. There were whispers in the hall; he was schizophrenic. He soon left.

Julius Caesar:
Three years of Latin made me more interested in him than in any figure except Jesus. Caesar, his campaigns, his armies, his assassination, the betrayal by Brutus on the steps of the Capitol. How I loved him.

Maybelle Hoffman:
The girl who created a sensation when she transferred to our high school from a town in southern Ohio . . . waist-length curly dark brown hair . . .

greenish eyes . . . olive-brown skin. She set a new standard of femininity for the rest of us to observe and aspire to. She flirted. She spoke in a whisper. She lost her books and had to borrow copies from the boys, and she wore Fatal Apple lipstick, which we all went downtown to May Co. and bought.

Eleanor Parker:
She was in the movie *Of Human Bondage*. Her father taught Geometry at our high school. We couldn't understand why Mr. Parker would want to teach Geometry when he had a daughter in the movies.

Flavius David:
He taught World History and was the first person whom I ever heard say that every event was connected to every other event. And that there was a "universal unconscious." All events are connected, he would say. I hurried along the corridor at nine in the morning and sat right in front of him. It was the most exciting class I'd ever had.

Moira Shearer, THE RED SHOES:
In high school I saw *The Red Shoes*. One day ten years later I would see it again at the Thalia in New York and see how the image of Vicki Page had been haunting me.

Mrs. Rosebaugh and Thisbe:
In my Latin production, I played Thisbe. That and winning the Latin Award for excellence are precious memories. And I got to wear another white robe (a sheet) just as Mary had worn. White nightgowns and robes, as well as the Palatine and a Latin classroom, found their way into my plays *A Rat's Mass* and *A Lesson in Dead Language*.

Mr. Tucker:
I could hardly wait to go to Choral Club. It met once a week in a charming music room with many windows and an oval stage. We in the Choral Club sat in long rows on seats that faced the stage, where Mr. Tucker stood in the center in a gray suit and vest next to the pianist, and taught us all the songs from Rodgers and Hammerstein's *Carousel*. "You'll Never Walk Alone" was our graduation song, a song that made us all cry.

Mr. Bloch (high school homeroom teacher):
He cried when we gave him a tie for his birthday and he cried on the day our class graduated. I wondered, did that mean he loved us? We loved him.

Laura (in THE GLASS MENAGERIE):
From my extreme empathy with her I learned that I too felt frightened and crippled, which was totally puzzling to me. Why? Why did I feel like Laura? Why? I was popular in high school, had a boyfriend and went out constantly with my friends to movies, picnics and the Friday-night Y canteen dance. Why?

COLLEGE
1 9 4 9 – 1 9 5 3

Fitzgerald
My husband-to-be
Willy Loman
Lorca

F. Scott Fitzgerald:
We read his stories in Freshman English at Ohio State in a class held in a Quonset hut. As it rained that winter quarter I was concerned because these stories, "The Diamond as Big as the Ritz," "The Ice Palace," "May Day," seemed to convey that there was tragedy that would come with being in my twenties, disappointments, confusion about the nature of love; a darkness would surface that had not been seen before.

My dorm mates at Ohio State:
Often from southern Ohio towns, they were determined to subjugate the Negro girls. They were determined to make you feel that it was a great inequity that they had to live in the same dorm with you . . . an injustice. This dark reality was later to give great impetus and energy to my dreams.

Jesse Owens:
Often when I was feeling lost in the huge classes at Ohio State, I thought of Jesse Owens. (His daughter lived in the next dorm and talked of him a great deal.) The image of Jesse Owens helped and sustained me in the immensity of the place.

My brother had run track in high school and came down to Ohio State briefly (hoping to run), but soon left. The immensity, the dark, rainy winters, the often open racial hatred of the girls in the dorm continued to demoralize me. I attached myself to my husband-to-be and seldom left his side.

Writers:
In the rainy winters we read Ezra Pound (he went insane). We read the furious prose of William Faulkner, we read Richard Wright's *Native Son* (Bigger Thomas killed a white woman) and "The Killers" by Heming-way. We were asked to analyze why Eliot's era was called the Age of Anxiety, we were asked to analyze why another time had been called the Lost Generation. How could a whole generation be lost, I thought. We were asked to understand that Fitzgerald's Jay Gatsby was a symbol for a generation. How

could these people speak for a whole generation? How wonderful, how marvelous they must be. These were living people, not dead like George Eliot or Shakespeare. These people lived in New York, Paris, Spain. Often they were exiles. They wandered just as Miss Edwards (in junior high) had told us that Shelley wandered. They fought wars, fell in love, were divorced, and most of all, we gathered in our dorm rooms to talk of them. These people were wonderful. These writers!

Myself:
My freshman year I took a few courses in social work but changed my major to Elementary Education in my second year, taking education courses like most of my friends. I halfheartedly studied them. But there was no wonder in them for me as in the English Lit courses inside the Quonset hut.

Elizabeth Taylor:
We saw Elizabeth Taylor in *A Place in the Sun*. I asked the hairdresser to try to cut my hair like Taylor's. We all wanted a formal dress like the one she wore when she danced with Montgomery Clift. "He loved her so much," I'd think, "he murdered."

Rodgers and Hammerstein:
Sometimes in the dorm we sang songs from *South Pacific*. And my roommate and I played the record in our room. I still often thought of MGM musicals.

We thought Jane Powell was adorable and saw *Royal Wedding*.

Joseph Kennedy:
My boyfriend. He told me about other places . . . Los Angeles, New York. He painted pictures of us traveling and belonging to a larger world. I listened to every word he said.

T. S. Eliot:
Because of *The Wasteland*, another work we read inside the Quonset hut a rainy winter at Ohio State, my idea changed as to what could be accomplished in poetry. These poems spoke for a whole generation.

Florence:
She read a magazine called *The New Yorker* every week and she spoke Spanish.

Marilyn Monroe:
We trudged up to High Street in the snow to see someone all the boys were talking of, in the movie *Niagara* . . .

Brando:
We went up to High Street to see him in *Streetcar Named Desire*.

Willy Loman:
I saw *Death of a Salesman*. Willy Loman was critical of life and he chose to die. I pondered—was it possible or acceptable to be critical of life? Was it possible that if a person felt cheated or miserable he could choose death?

In the dormitory at Ohio State all we talked of was clothes, our boyfriends, parties. Yet both my parents had at times told me they were not happy. Were they unhappy like Willy Loman? Did people grow sadder as they grew older? I wasn't sad. I was engaged to be married.

Myself and my engagement ring:
How enchanted I was with my engagement ring and my engagement. I'm engaged, I said to everyone. When my fiancé and I were together I knew I had found the Blue Bird of Happiness.

Lorca:
My friend Florence, who majored in Spanish, gave me *Poet in New York* to read. My unhappiness with the racial climate at Ohio State and the drafting of my fiancé into the army left me feeling dark. Lorca's dark complex vision was thrilling and comforting to me.

Florence told me Lorca had been killed mysteriously. The year before,

I had seen *Death of a Salesman*. These writers said tragedy was the nature of life. There was a crosscurrent in life that moved across football games, dances, clothes, worries over our possible silver patterns and wedding dresses.

My husband and a journey:
"We'll go to New York and live when we marry," he said. I realized that would be a journey.

Myself:
Three weeks before my graduation, Joe and I married. He was being shipped off to Colorado by the army. I was to join him in Colorado the Monday after my graduation. So eager . . . so desperate to be with him again that I hardly realized I was ending my college years. I was a bride going off to live in Denver with my husband. That's all I could think of.

MARRIAGE AND MOTHERHOOD
1953 – 1960

Dreaming of being a writer
More of Williams, Lorca, Chekhov,
  many others and myself
And still remembering childhood . . .

The United States Army (1953):
We were newly married, happy in Colorado for six months until the army intervened. The army caused me to enter a state of anxiety I had never known before by sending my husband to Korea. Now I was pregnant. "Can't I go?" I begged. "I could live nearby." But off he went. We were separated for a year . . . the year of the birth of our child.

Myself:
When I was back home with my parents, pregnant, waiting for my husband to come back from Korea, I used to browse in a magical bookstore called Shroeder's in Cleveland's Public Square. It was there I discovered a magazine called *Theatre Arts*. In it was a photograph of Williams and Kazan backstage at *Streetcar Named Desire* and also an essay by Williams on writing. He spoke of Michelangelo, of Cézanne, and how he studied their paintings. He spoke of Anton Chekhov. I read *Streetcar Named Desire* and made a plan to read Chekhov. It was then, that winter, that I sat in my parents' living room and wrote my first play. For some reason, I set it in New York, perhaps because I was so looking forward to going to New York when my husband returned from Korea.

My mother:
Now, just as I had married, my mother spoke increasingly of the difficulties of that state.

Tennessee Williams:

While I was pregnant I read as much of Williams as possible. *Streetcar Named Desire* was at the height of its fame. My friends and I were in love with Marlon Brando (from his films) and saw Brando as a rebel; he was the first movie star (in the dorm) that both my white and my Negro friends had loved equally, at a time when we seemed to have little in common except our passion for "engagements" and engagement rings. And weddings.

Marlon Brando as rebel:

Rebellion was an abstraction to me. I knew perfectly well what my life was to be and I was very happy with it. My husband would finish graduate school at Columbia, which he had started before he went to Korea. We would have two or three children and live in a suburb. Yet the myth of Brando fascinated me. You live in a "walk-up," you wear T-shirts, you disdain social events, you criticize society—this picture of the creative person was possibly the most powerful picture I had since I was twelve and saw *Song to Remember*, the life of Chopin (a great composer was sickly, nervous, erratic and dark in mood and lived in romantic surroundings). These ideas of "creative people" were affecting me far more deeply than I realized. Often I now thought, how could I be a part of this world where people were called "creative" and became famous?

Movie stars:

When I was pregnant (and waiting for my husband to return from Korea) sometimes I dreamed of being a movie star. (Perhaps I could study acting with Stella Adler like Marlon Brando.) But I couldn't figure out what roles I would play. If I were an actress I would want to play roles like Bette Davis's. I abandoned that idea and started to write a play.

JULIUS CAESAR:

I saw the movie with Louis Calhern, Brando and James Mason. I bought the recording of the movie and played it for my father. He seemed subdued these days and sometimes (in the evening) looked at his scrapbooks of '30s newspaper clippings of himself. Hearing of Caesar will help, I thought.

struggling along in an
t building that was an
settlement house 17 years

s first week in Cleveland,
vandered through the
s district, saw sights that
with concern and sad-
children, seeking chan-
is curiosity and energy,
groups at street corners.
rected adolescent groups
paths of delinquency,
realized that parents
ss to better the circum-
? decided his first job
the friendship, confi-
ie children.
t a shiny black bat, a
catcher's mit and mask.
quipment he strolled into

Olivier:

My mother and I went to see *Carrie* (based on Dreiser's book). She still had a crush on Olivier. And she still cried at the movies. By now (unlike in the '30s) so did I.

Myself:

It was while my husband was in Korea that I sometimes began to daydream of being a writer, perhaps a famous writer.

My father (again):

By now he was assistant head of Race Relations in Cleveland. His office was in City Hall, and when I went to visit him in Cleveland I climbed the palatial white steps and entered the grand foyer of City Hall. How proud I was.

Our son Joe . . . his birth:

My husband:

He returned from Korea. How happy I was. I took the train to New York and met him under the clock at Grand Central Station.

My new family:

Joe was to continue graduate school. We settled in an apartment building called Bancroft, on 121st Street between Broadway and Amsterdam, a building for married students. I was very anxious, but hardly aware of it. It was the beginning of a decade of discovery.

My husband Joe:

How he focused his energy, ignoring fatigue, and how he refused to acknowledge obstacles, but just continued to work hard at goals. He made working hard seem like an adventure.

Myself, New York:

Sometimes when I'd walk down the street I'd hum "I Like New York in June." What a wonderful place! Perhaps if I wore more eye makeup I'd look like Audrey Hepburn. Everything seemed to happen to her. What magical streets, Central Park West, Central Park South, Fifth Avenue (where Fred Astaire and Judy Garland had walked in the Easter Parade), Best and Co., Saks, Rockefeller Center, NBC.

I bought black toreador pants and a black sweater and gathered my hair in a ponytail—like Audrey Hepburn and the girls in *Vogue*—and I daydreamed.

I started another play, about a family—the father was a minister and they lived in a kind of biblical setting. . . .

I started another play about a family . . . perhaps the father could give fine stirring sermons . . . perhaps the mother could have dense complex dreams and wake with circles under her eyes . . . I tried to capture this.

Yet I still didn't really understand how intensely I wanted my family on the stage (like the family in *Our Town*), like Tom, Laura and Amanda in *The Glass Menagerie*.

My brother:
Often I'd still think of us with our decoder rings, sitting by the Philco radio waiting for a message from Jack Armstrong.

My father:
Reading *Blondie and Dagwood* to me.

Judy Garland:
Singing "Have Yourself a Merry Little Christmas" or "The Trolley Song."

Mr. David:
Often I thought of his saying, "All events are connected!"

Joan and her mother:
And I still thought of them reading *The Cherry Orchard* aloud to each other on a sunny summer afternoon.

And I remembered Aldonna Kelly:
The most envied girl in junior high (by white and Negro kids alike) for her waist-length blond hair and green eyes at a moment when I thought I looked "icky."

People my husband and I met at gatherings around Columbia University:
They never asked me about anything: They said, how's the baby? They asked my husband about his graduate studies in Social Psychology, his opinion of the world and politics. As an afterthought they most often, but pleasantly, asked me, how's the baby? How old is the baby? Do you like New York? I resolved to work harder at my writing and to take courses.

My mother:
She sent us small checks and often bought the baby his fall or spring outfits.

Emily Dickinson:

I read her poems and I read of her life. It seemed that if you had a garden and wore white dresses it helped in becoming an immortal poetess. Famous writers often seemed to be powerful images in themselves.

I remembered Joan:

And her telling me of "great Russian writers," and I bought *Crime and Punishment* and *The Brothers Karamazov*. They were vivid red volumes with red silk markers. When I read them I felt I was inside the blood of the Russian characters.

My son Joe:

Reading him stories (Milne, Lear) and watching him play games in his cowboy suit, or his Mouseketeer hat, or sitting in his Indian tent engaged my imagination and provided a constant example of how real the unreal is. It was all a moving example of how people (from early childhood) naturally take on other identities.

My son Joe:

Caring for him in dark winter twilight hours or on long summer days by its solitary nature helped me to become perhaps more myself than I had ever been. The books I read while sitting in Riverside Park, *Crime and Punishment*, Gorki's *Childhood*, burned deeply in my mind in contrast to the kaffeeklatsch conversations of the other young mothers. My husband had an immense study-and-work schedule and we were in this strange new city of New York. All of this, because it left me more on my own than I'd ever been before, caused my mind to leap and tumble in many chasms, good and bad. Even the current jargon fit—people talked of women with small children as being in "the icebox years" and they discussed Reisman's *The Lonely Crowd*. Was I in "the icebox years"? I wondered as I went to the tiny supermarket on Amsterdam Ave. Was I part of "the lonely crowd"? I thought as I went to the laundromat or chatted with the other young mothers. Away from my childhood community of Cleveland, these thoughts began to occupy my mind more and more. Had Emma Bovary felt she was in "the icebox years" when she fled the care of her child for love affairs? Did Raskolnikov in *Crime and Punishment* feel part of "the lonely crowd"? For the first time, at age twenty-four, I wondered how I fit in—anywhere.

Verdi's AÏDA:
My husband and I saw it at the Amato Opera House on Bleecker Street with Mr. Amato conducting. The small opera house was enchanting, and Verdi provided me with an Egyptian heroine.

Princess Zinaida (in Turgenev's "First Love"):
A heroine who possessed an essential romanticism that I could not seem to convey in my heroines on the New York landscape or the Ohio landscape— to yearn, to dream, to be in love, even tragically in love, as the Princess Zinaida was. But she was a countess living in the idyllic Russian summer landscape. How would I transfer that lyricism to the heroines in my stories? It seemed futile. For a start I bought a pale green stone necklace at a store on MacDougal Street and a pale green shirtwaist dress to match (from the Grab Bag on Broadway) and dreamed of being in Turgenev's Russia as I walked down Broadway taking my son to play in Riverside Park.

RASHOMON (I saw the movie again):
It haunted me by its mystery. Life is like that, I thought: human visions crossing, disputing one another, violently clashing.

Louis Armstrong:
We saw him at Lewisohn Stadium—a performer I had as much affection for as for a member of my family.

My father (again, in the '50s):
Life had begun to merge with literature. My father had by now changed from an outgoing gregarious man to a Hamlet . . . a Willy Loman. He reflected, pondered constantly the meaning of his past life. So now I had "two fathers"—my heroic father of the '30s and '40s and now my Hamlet–Willy Loman father of the '50s. I tried to reconcile them . . . but it tormented me.

Eugene O'Neill:
I'll be forever grateful to him for the extraordinary light he shed on the matrix of his family relationships in *Long Day's Journey into Night*, the greatest play I had seen on the stage, with Jason Robards, Fredric March, Florence Eldridge and Bradford Dillman, directed by José Quintero and produced by Theodore Mann and Circle in the Square.

Maxim Gorki:
His *Childhood.*

Jason Robards and Eugene O'Neill, THE ICEMAN COMETH:
The play at Circle in the Square on Sheridan Square remains to this day the second-greatest experience I have had in the theater. Seeing what would become historic productions (*Iceman* and *Long Day's Journey*) made it clear the stage was where mysterious, unparalleled passion and dilemmas of the deepest kind could be expressed. I was torn between my own slight stories and a play I had been struggling with for two years, and which I dreamily envisioned at Circle in the Square off Sheridan Square. I worked even harder at creating settings. My settings seemed so pallid, so weak in comparison to these two plays which now haunted my mind.

Emma Bovary and Anna Karenina:
In my sneakers and toreador pants or skirt and sweater left over from college, I often felt caring for a baby all day and being a young housewife a tremendous letdown. Was this where my life had been leading? I seemed drab to myself. The people I read about seemed to be leading thrilling lives. I first found comfort in my state of mind from reading *Madame Bovary.* Emma was married to a doctor. She had a small child. And yet she felt unfulfilled, restless, unhappy. I tried to find answers in the pages of Flaubert. The problem was that my feelings were dispersed, vague, illogical. Often I reread a book on Marie Curie. Many times I felt so unfulfilled in my role as a young "housewife" that Emma's taking arsenic made sense to me. I felt I also understood Anna Karenina's unhappiness. Both these women were plagued by endless, mysterious feelings of unhappiness and confusion despite the fact that they found a certain joy in their children and marriages. They were in an inexplicable turmoil, as I was.

Victoria Page and THE RED SHOES (the romantic, beautiful ballerina):
It is clear now that it was Jane Eyre (the child) I identified with, and the growing young woman's dilemmas of the Bette Davis character in *Now, Voyager,* but it was Victoria Page in *The Red Shoes* whom I most dreamed of becoming as an adult.

The trouble with Vicki Page and the troubling aspect of assuming her persona was that she killed herself by jumping off a balcony onto a speeding train. This definitely created and left me with a problem. How was I to complete my adult life?

Yet, still, I went on buying dresses as close as possible to the teal shade of blue of the dress that Vicki Page wore the evening she climbed the steps to Lermontov's villa and he told her he would create a dance for her . . . *The Red Shoes*. Perhaps I thought if I wore my blue dresses I would meet a Lermontov who would create a dance for me.

(Years later I would wear an evening dress of the same color to the opening night of my first produced play.)

But *then* I continued to imagine that one day I would meet a Lermontov and he would recognize me (as Victoria Page) and suddenly my entire life would be transformed and I would live within a vibrant world of romance and glamour.

Chekhov, Dante, Virgil and the Bible:
Over and over I copied passages from them, studying the language and the rhythms.

Chekhov and my brother:
I saw my brother and myself as Nina and Constantine in *The Seagull*. My brother was in the army now and unhappy. As a child he had drawn countless pictures of soldiers, angular stick figures killing each other, engaged in war battles, in tanks, on battlefields. The pencil drawings on notebook paper of soldiers falling, shooting, climbing had an odd intensity that was in contrast to my brother's sweet face, his sandy hair and huge brown eyes.

Sometimes I thought of his drawings as my mother confided to me how much he hated the army and Germany. Maybe it was because Constantine had shot himself that I sensed something terrible would happen. Although it was still years before his automobile accident, coma and eventual death.

I remembered—

My parents' hometown (1930s):
Montezuma, Georgia, looked to me like the drawings we were given in Sunday school of Jerusalem, the golden and red and white colors of the landscape, the processions of people walking on the road coming from the fields, walking to church (winding roads, view of steeples).

Our neighborhood, Cleveland:
Our immigrant and Negro neighborhood with its small frame houses or brick double houses with small square yards in Mount Pleasant seemed so far away from the romance of *The Secret Garden* or *Jane Eyre* that I began to read even more to connect myself to it.

People my parents talked about:
Looming very large were the people my parents talked about after they sent me outside to play. Sometimes I would at least hear part of their names. And when we'd go to church I'd find myself staring at so-and-so who I knew had that first name; what had they done that made my mother whisper on the phone, or caused me to be sent outside to play so it could be talked about? Often they'd say, "No one really knows the truth, but people say . . ." Contradictory voices, different versions of a story as a way of penetrating to the truth of things, would become important in my work.

Beethoven (1956):
I ordered all his string quartets from a record club. Each record was wrapped in delicate paper and the record covers were in romantic pale colors. How I treasured them.

Joe:
For more than a decade he read every word I wrote and encouraged me to continue.

John Selby:
My writing teacher at Columbia. He said I "might be touched with genius" and gave my novel to his publishing house.

Leonard Lyons:
For a decade I yearned to be in his *New York Post* column.

Napoleon:
From Corsica he saw the coast of France and dreamed of conquest. A great

dream has to come before great achievement, was what I learned from reading his biography.

Beethoven:

His string quartets taught me that dark, impossible, unbearable moods could be transposed into work. A creative person could capture what he felt in andante, allegro, molta bella.

Van Gogh:

An artist can feel intense isolation.

Beethoven:

A creative person can look forward to capturing his life in these forms, a creative person can look forward to giving life meaning.

Debussy:

Melodies could comfort.

Eric Dolphy, Dizzy Gillespie, Count Basie, Duke Ellington, Louis Armstrong, Joe Williams, Charlie Mingus, Miles Davis:

All of whom I actually saw and heard perform. Inspiration!

All the Elizabeths (English):

Women who had whole epochs named after them. That meant I must keep trying to rise above shopping at the supermarket, gossiping with other young mothers. I was a woman too. I must try to achieve.

Greek heroines:

Antigone, Electra. Their vision was chronicled for me to share two thousand years later. Then the conflicts in women were important. I wasn't being weak or cowardly to often feel the same distress and conflicts. I made them my friends. Nothing I felt was wrong, since they had felt it centuries before me.

Giotto:

By my mid-twenties the colors of life had shifted dangerously. I saw a great deal of trouble in people around me, people whom I loved. Friends, family told me their troubles, wept, were often bitter, said they didn't want to go on. I tried to write of it.

One day, I stumbled on a book of Giotto prints: the colors, the violet blues, the magentas, moss greens, matching my growing vision of the world. I cut out the prints, put them above my desk and tried to use the colors in my poems and stories.

Mildred Kuner:
My teacher at the New School, 1955. She got excited about my first play and entered it in a contest at Chapel Hill.

Edward Mabley:
My teacher at the American Theatre Wing. When I dropped out of the class because I was too shy to "talk" when the plays were discussed, he wrote me a postcard that said, I hope you'll come back to class. I like your writing very much.

Thornton Wilder:
I still thought of Emily from *Our Town*. And at the same time I would think of our high school class. I was not yet aware of how much I missed high school and the close friends, going to the Y dances, eating Boston cream pie in the lunchroom and then going to the daily movie (for two cents) in the school auditorium, sitting together giggling over *Margie*, learning "It's a Grand Night for Singing" in Choral Club.

Richard Wright:
I often tried to imagine his life in Paris.

My brother-in-law and famous people:
He'd met many famous people, entertainers, athletes, people who were in Leonard Lyons' column. Famous people began to appear to be people that "people knew." I was amazed by that.

Myself and psalms:
I continued to read psalms often to quell the fear I felt at seeing the strange, fragmented thoughts that poured from my diaries, the violent imagery. Why so violent? I didn't understand. I had many black moods. And would cry for no apparent reason.

Marlon Brando:
His roles seemed to convey themes.
    In *Viva Zapata*, a person has to fight and lead.
    In *Streetcar*, there is within the world violence, danger.
    In *On the Waterfront*, a person must try to attain honor.

Cézanne:
(I was given a book of the Impressionists.) There is strength and symmetry within our physical environment that can support us.

Sibelius (FINLANDIA):
Pride and devotion to one's land are to be desired.

Monet:
Within our physical world there is everlasting beauty.

Dostoevsky:
Severe trauma and trial are natural to our existence.

Wordsworth:
Memory and longing for the past are with us daily.

Audrey Wood (literary agent):
The play I wrote at the New School (*The Pale Blue Flowers*) got me my first letter from a literary agent. Although she didn't take me on, she wrote a long encouraging letter. I was only twenty-four. So her letter was important. After all, she was Tennessee Williams' agent.

Lillian Hellman:
She was a woman and a playwright. She had created *The Little Foxes*, which became a movie with another Bette Davis role I loved.

Mrs. Rosebaugh and Caesar (mid-'50s):
I bought a book at a bookstore on 116th and Broadway. It had a passage Mrs. Rosebaugh had read to us many times in high school Latin class. The book was called *Caesar's War Commentaries*: "Gaul consists of three distinct regions inhabited respectively by the Belgae, the Aquitani and a people who call themselves Celt but are known to us as Galli." She had read in Latin and then translated into English, her frail voice trembling. The sound of Mrs. Rosebaugh reading Latin is a sound I today strive for when I write, just as I strive for the emotional levels of spirituals. Nobody Knows the Trouble I've Seen, Nobody Knows but Jesus. And, Sometimes I Feel Like

a Motherless Child. And, Go Down Moses, Way Down to Egypt Land, Tell Old Pharaoh to Let My People Go.

Bette Davis in Now, Voyager:
In this avid dream of transformation I still also daydreamed of myself as this character. She was plain. She was troubled. She was controlled by her mother and then one day she took a trip on an ocean liner and total fulfillment came to her because of this trip on the ocean. She became beautiful and loved. One day I'm going to take a trip on an ocean liner, I thought, and all my dark thoughts and feelings, all my feelings that I don't belong anywhere, will go away.

D. H. Lawrence (Sons and Lovers):
Lawrence's use of landscape was something that I worked feverishly at accomplishing in my own work but was never able to achieve. Reading Lawrence made me highly aware of my inability to capture sweeping landscapes on paper as much as I longed to. I was aware of the impossibility of capturing them.

I remembered—

My mother (again)—*her red scrapbook from the '20s:*
Sometimes I think I see life as like my mother's red scrapbook which held and still holds today a powerful fascination—the book of sepia-colored photographs (which still sits in our attic) of my parents and their friends in Atlanta, when they all were young, is a constant reminder of the elusive nature of life.

Emma Bovary, James Baldwin and Proust
   (1950s):
I bought a beautiful map of France at Macy's to see if I could trace their separate comings and goings in France.

    Emma Bovary had traveled to see Léon. James Baldwin lived and trav-

eled in France. (I carried his book *Notes of a Native Son* in my purse.) And Proust had constantly traveled through the French countryside. My map was painted in vivid colors on papyruslike paper. I treasured it.

Book on Socrates:
I underlined the passage:

> According to Plato, Socrates had been struck by the Orphic doctrine that there are means by which the soul can be restored to remembrance of her forgotten divine origin, that the acquisition of knowledge generally is in reality . . . a process of "recollection" or recognition . . . *anamnesis.*

Nina (in THE SEAGULL):
In my wild, desperate attempts to become a writer I felt like Nina in the first act of Chekhov's *The Seagull* when she and Constantine staged their amateurish play . . . so desperate to express my thoughts and feelings . . . her speech spoke for me.

"I am alone. Once in a hundred years I open my lips to speak and my voice echoes mournfully in the void and no one hears . . . like a prisoner . . ."

I now had a group of five stories making the rounds of magazines. None found a publisher. I started a new novel, mostly writing late at night, consuming coffee. People continued to talk about how talented I was.

Nellie Rosebaugh:
Often I'd think of my high school Latin teacher. She told us, "Caesar led a great life . . . greatness is possible in man. Man can be epic. Man can be noble."

My parents and New York:
Often I'd remember that New York was where my parents had spent their honeymoon, at the Hotel Theresa, and had gone to a nightclub called the Big Apple.

Our friends:

We talked about Frank Sinatra (we still wanted him to go back to Nancy), Mike Todd and Elizabeth Taylor. We wondered did Marlon Brando love Anna Kashfi and we talked about Charlie Mingus and Miles Davis, and Billie Holiday.

Josephine Baker, Mabel Mercer:

I reflected on these Negro women whom I had read about. (Mabel Mercer we would soon see at the Byline Room.) They had gone to Europe to be "discovered." Was that a necessity? By now, the late 1950s, my husband was finished with grad school and teaching at a New York college. We lived on 95th Street, only a few doors from Central Park West. And when we walked outside we could see the trees on Central Park West. It was wonderful. Nights we'd walk in the park.

Our friends:

Many of our friends were by now "seeing analysts." We enjoyed talking about our depressions, the movie *Breathless*, Eric Dolphy, Charlie Mingus and Miles Davis. The magazines were filled with photographs of new Kennedy babies and the perfect life they all led. And one of America's most famous writers married Marilyn Monroe. We talked about that a lot. We talked about James Baldwin and Norman Mailer.

Willy Loman:

By now I had reread *Death of a Salesman* many times. And I was still concerned about Willy and his lapse into madness and suicide. I wrote down in my notebooks what Arthur Miller said in interviews about writing.

Winston Churchill and myself:

My husband admired the many dimensions of Churchill's career: author, statesman, soldier. I often wondered how I, as a woman, could have a "destiny" (like Churchill). Careers connected with great destiny all seemed to be for men. It didn't seem possible that I would be a Marie Curie or a Marian Anderson or an Eleanor Roosevelt. I couldn't fly a plane like Amelia Earhart, I didn't feel I could change society like Mary Bethune or Helen Keller. Although I had stories, poems and one and a half novels and a play, was I even capable of being an author? I wanted a "destiny." But no one seemed to see me in this light. At twenty-six, even though I had studied for two years at Columbia General Studies writing my novel and had gone to the New School and had tried to read my way through the Modern Library and had acquired an agent at MCA, people still (very often) asked me only: Would I like to help plan the kindergarten Halloween party? Would I be part of a group of mothers taking the kindergarteners to the Boat Pond in Central Park? I seemed bland and mediocre to myself. I often felt miserable. I told my husband. "Keep writing," he said.

People in VOGUE:
I pored over every page of this magazine and dreamed of being in its pages.

Tennessee Williams:
The writer whose career and plays I coveted. It took ten years to stop imitating him, to stop using his form and to stop stealing his themes, which were not mine.

Truman Capote:
Capote's short stories, like "Miriam," and those in *Other Voices, Other Rooms*, seemed perfection to me. Capote in Russia, Capote in Paris, Capote interviewing Brando, Capote working with John Huston, Capote on Broadway, *House of Flowers*, Capote on television. *The Grass Harp*. If only I could have a life like that, I thought.

James Agee:
I memorized what Agee thought about "film."

Dylan Thomas:
We bought his poetry on a record and played it at parties. How strange it seemed that a Welsh poet should die at St. Vincent's Hospital on 12th Street.

Jung:
Dreams, memories. I must stop trying to ignore
them.

Kazan, Williams, Brando:
Would I ever be part of an artistic brotherhood like
this? Ever?

The Wolf Man:
He still held a power over me. Metamorphosis and
change of identity would become a theme that
would dominate my writing. Soon the characters
in my plays and stories would be changing personae
at an alarming rate.

Kazan:
He was like Michelangelo to me. The pictures he
painted on the screen, *Viva Zapata*, *On the Water-
front*, *East of Eden*, made me crazy and restless.

Sidney Poitier:
An extraordinarily handsome "Negro" man whom
I could watch up on the screen just as I could watch
Newman and Lancaster.

Virgil (1957):
Passage I read from Virgil each morning before I started to write, while studying with John Selby:

> I sing of arms and the man who came of old, a fated wanderer from the coasts of Troy to Italy and the shore of Lavinium; hard driven on land and on the deep by the violence of heaven, by reason of cruel Juno's unforgetful anger . . .

I yearned for my writing to have this texture.

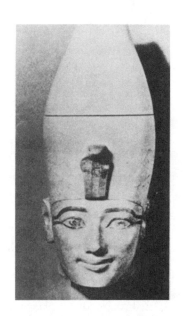

Beethoven and Hatshepsut:
I'd often stare at the statue of Beethoven I kept on the left-hand side of my desk. I felt it contained a "secret." I'd do the same with the photograph of Queen Hatshepsut that was on the wall. I did *not* then understand that I felt torn between these forces of my ancestry . . . European and African . . . a fact that would one day explode in my work.

Beethoven and Hatshepsut (again):
When friends asked me about my statue, my collection of postcards, my photographs of people, I always said they were inspirational. I did not see that they were so much more. Soon I *would* understand that I was in a dialogue with the photographs, prints, postcards of people. They were my alter egos.

Duchess of Hapsburg (JUAREZ):
In the Paul Muni movie I saw at the Symphony, I was struck by the Duchess of Hapsburg as played by Bette Davis. In 1957 my husband, son and I visited Chapultepec Palace, where the Hapsburgs had lived. I bought many postcards of the palace and the Duchess of Hapsburg and saved them. One day the Duchess of Hapsburg would become one of my characters' most sympathetic alter egos or selves.

At the time in Mexico there seemed something amiss about European royalty living amid the Aztec culture. European royalty in an alien landscape. Soon my Duchess of Hapsburg would exist in an alien persona, that of the character of the Negro writer.

Some other movie characters who haunted me:
Shelley Winters in *A Place in the Sun*, the essence of longing.
    Montgomery Clift in *A Place in the Sun*, a yearning to belong.
    Marlon Brando in *Viva Zapata*, an ideal of nobility . . . of sensuality.
    Jean Peters in *Viva Zapata*, an ideal of feminine beauty.
    (These people would become characters in a play called *A Movie Star Has to Star in Black and White*, a play in which the movie fantasies of the heroine overshadow her life.)

I still thought of:
    Spirituals
    Our family at camp
    My brother and me during the War
    Billie Holiday

I remembered—

Negro spirituals and myself (1930s):
I had a slim yellow book on the piano that contained many Negro spirituals, "Go Down, Moses," "Sometimes I Feel like a Motherless Child," "Nobody Knows the Trouble I've Seen," "He Knows Just How Much We Can Bear."

My mother often sang when she cooked Sunday-morning breakfast: particularly "Sometimes I Feel like a Motherless Child." It seemed that we as "Negroes" sang of sorrow. It seemed strange. In the church in Georgia that my cousins and I drove in the carriage to, the songs were even sadder. They were moans. Why did we "sing" of sorrow?

Our family at camp:
My father was the Y camp director in the 1930s and took us all to camp with him. The camp was a lovely place called Centerville Mills, in a rolling green

Ohio landscape. Together we climbed the grassy hill to the cottage with its hooked rugs and Early American furniture, together we went to the Chapel-in-the-Woods and together we sang in the dining hall and by the campfire.

My brother and me during the War:
My mother worked at the War plant on Sundays. Everything was different, so now on Sundays my brother and I rode the Kinsman streetcar downtown to the Palace Theatre and saw people like Cab Calloway, Nat King Cole and Lionel Hampton. I in my wedgies, gloves and hat, my brother in long pants, shirt and tie. After the show my father picked us up in the Plymouth.

Federico García Lorca (POET IN NEW YORK, 1950s):
This book, like all of Lorca's work, showed me that imagery is multilayered, that it comes from recovering connections long ago lost and buried.

William Faulkner:
He reinforced what I, as a child, had felt in my visits to Georgia to see my grandparents: that the South was a strange mesh of dark kinship between the races.

James Baldwin (Notes of a Native Son):
He sharpened my entire vision of America.

Gwendolyn Brooks (Maude Martha):
She caused me to examine many subliminal feelings and gave me a Negro heroine, Maude Martha, against whom I could measure myself. Brooks herself was a role model, for she was a poet who had won the Pulitzer Prize.

Anne Frank (on seeing the Broadway play with
   Susan Strasberg, one Thanksgiving afternoon):
I cried aloud in the theater when the Germans came up the stairs to the annex. It was the evil of Hitler again.

Elizabeth Taylor:
If you're beautiful, the whole world can be yours. And feminine beauty is an *achievement*.

England, *where Du Maurier lived.*

Daphne Du Maurier:
When I was twenty-five, I saw a photograph of Du Maurier at home in England in the Sunday *Times*. She sat in her study, at a large desk by a window. I arranged my desk as much like hers as possible, close to our windows, and I tried often to strike a Du Maurier-like pose.

Wagner:
The music in the Ring Cycle which I saw at the old Metropolitan Opera House expressed a wild intensity that I felt growing inside me, but that I could not explain or comprehend.

Modern Library:
All the people in the pages of the books that I read.

Picasso:
After I saw *Guernica* at the Museum of Modern Art, the concept of placing my characters in a dream domain seemed more and more real to me.

Jackson Pollock:
After seeing his work at the Museum of Modern Art, I thought continually of how to write (was it possible?) without a linear narrative.

Frank Lloyd Wright:
His diaries, which I discovered in a bookstore on Morningside Heights, convinced me that I must work harder to formulate the goals I was trying to achieve in my writing, and work harder at dissecting the components of this form. I had to read more and analyze music, writing and painting. I had to read criticism, I couldn't rely on accident.

Constantine (in Chekhov's THE SEAGULL):
I loved him. He couldn't get his mother's attention. He shot himself.

André Maurois:
His biography of Proust provided me with a detailed account of Proust's life as he wrote. For the first time I was able to visualize the process of a writer's working relationship to his social life, his friendships, his family and his illnesses. Before reading this book, I had found the process of being a writer vague and mysterious. From this profound biography I was also able to understand how Proust selected material (from society, life, friends) and transformed it into his vision.

My brother Cornell (again, the '50s): I wasn't aware of it, but many times when I read and reread Chekhov's *The Seagull* I saw my brother as Constantine. (If my brother and I could only play jacks again and bounce the tiny red ball on the porch. If we could only play pick-up-sticks again or together with a piece of chalk draw hopscotch on the sidewalk in front of our house.) In his twenties my brother spoke bitterly of his life in a way I could not fathom. He often said he felt hopeless, and then he joined the army. Like Constantine, he seemed to feel an inability to get the esteem and attention he craved from the world . . . all the more puzzling to me because in many ways I had seen my brother as the favorite child.

Simone de Beauvoir and Jean-Paul Sartre:
They were models of brilliance, love and devotion (the Curies again). I often cut out pictures of them attending a world literary conference or sitting with

a group of students at a university in Paris. Sartre's *No Exit* was a short play that I often read.

Françoise Sagan:
She was said to have written *Bonjour Tristesse* in a month on her vacation, and now she was the toast of the literary world and an international celebrity. I pored curiously over its pages. And I felt depressed. I had already spent two years writing a novel in my workshop at Columbia.

Anne Frank (again):
I thought of her a great deal. Her life seemed a study in courage in adversity. I often thought of that attic in Amsterdam.

Psalms:
Before I wrote in the afternoon when my son was napping or in the evening when my husband was in the library at Columbia studying, I often read psalms. I read them many times, not only for inspiration but because I sensed that the characters in my stories yearned to speak of the world on the levels of the psalms (about what troubled them). I did not remember then, as I did years later, that often in the kitchen on winter evenings before dinner (after *Stella Dallas*) my mother had read me psalms. Often in later years, when I would hear an actress speaking the monologues from *Funnyhouse of a Negro* or *The Owl Answers*, I saw the fascinating mystical connection. My characters had the same emotional tone that my mother had possessed when over the porcelain kitchen table she had read to me from the Bible.

I remembered—

My Aunt Martha (my mother's half-sister):
She lived with us in her last two years of high school. She was from Georgia, pretty with freckles and brown curly hair. She read to me from *Romeo and Juliet*, which they were studying in her senior year, and told me she was also reading Shakespeare's sonnets.

Sometimes, quite suddenly, she would say:

"Shall I compare thee to a summer's day?
Thou art more lovely and more temperate:

Rough winds do shake the darling buds of May,
And summer's lease hath all too short a date."

and then announce, "That's Shakespeare."

She seldom had time to talk to me because she had to study. Everyone said she was "very smart." She was always introduced to my parents' friends as being "very smart," so smart she had been sent from a small town in Georgia to Cleveland to go to high school. She caused people to be silent and stare at her because she said things that were "beyond her years." When I thought no one was looking, I tried to read her books, and sometimes, if I was quiet enough, she would let me study with her. She was in her senior high school play, *The Barretts of Wimpole Street*.

✳ ✳ ✳

TANNHÄUSER *and Miss Clements* (1950s):
Miss Clements had told us of *Tannhäuser* and how Wagner captured Tannhäuser's longing with power, and I bought a book of Wagner librettos. My stories seemed so lacking in power that I thought studying these librettos might help. I tried to write five hours a day and was often exhausted.

Tannhäuser had longed for home. What I did not understand was that, however exhilarated I was by the discovery of New York, I too longed for home, for Ohio. Very often I carried the book of librettos with me. It was even crimson, the color of the book of Shelley poems, the color of my mother's scrapbook.

Virginia Woolf:
She drowned herself in a pond. How haunted by that I was.

Virginia Woolf:
From *To the Lighthouse*: "He had been to Amsterdam, Mr. Barkes was saying as he strolled across the lawn with Lily Briscoe. He had seen the Rembrandts." This illuminated the continual problem of capturing the elusive in my work. Would I ever be able to do so as Woolf could?

Montgomery Clift:
Next to Brando, the actor I admired most; but I sensed underneath his beauty something altogether frightening. (*From Here to Eternity, A Place in the Sun.*)

Emerson:
His essays sustained me, particularly "Circles" and "Self-Reliance." To believe in your thought, to believe that what is true for you in your own thought is true for all men, that is genius. . . . Trust thyself; every heart vibrates to that iron string. Accept the place the divine providence has found for you. . . .

People in the musicals:
Pajama Game, South Pacific, Oklahoma, Allegro, Guys and Dolls and *My Fair Lady.* (They had a sublime quality.)

Audrey Hepburn:
A role model in her portrayal of intelligent, intuitive young women.

Dorothy Dandridge:
I yearned to look like her—perhaps to be her.

Richard Wright (NATIVE SON):
As an exiled writer who lived in France, Wright provided for me an immeasurable personal symbol, a powerful Negro artist.

Racine:
His heroine, Phaedra.

Socrates:
The concept of Socrates in prison drinking hemlock fired my imagination. Why was a great thinker imprisoned?

Vincent Van Gogh:
His letters to his brother, Theo: "At one moment the scene is more tangled and fantastic than a thorn hedge, so confused that one finds no rest for the

eyes and gets giddy, is forced by the whirling of colors and lines to look first here, then there . . ."

Langston Hughes (again):
The Negro Speaks of Rivers . . . (his poem).

Aristotle (POETICS):
"The greatest thing by far is to be a master of metaphor. It is the one thing that cannot be learned for another and it is also a sign of genius since a good metaphor implies an intuitive perception of the similarity in dissimilars."

OLIVER TWIST (Charles Dickens):
Life can be an arduous journey, but it can end brilliantly.

Ben Franklin (on reading his autobiography):
He went abroad for self-discovery.

My friend Rachel (again):
She could recite Ronsard in French.

H. G. Wells:
His *History of the World* clarified how I might attack the problem of depicting my characters' personal histories.

Movies:
The Best Years of Our Lives, A Place in the Sun, Giant and the directors William Wyler and George Stevens.

Tennessee Williams:
His comments on the nature of writing and drama in the press and *Theatre Arts* magazine, especially an essay on how he utilized the colors of great painters in his work, and as well, actual scenes. He spoke of how he used a setting in Cézanne for inspiration as a scene in *Streetcar Named Desire*.

Hemingway:
He seemed an entire universe in himself . . . his books were films . . . the characters in his books were as famous as he was. Tales of his adventures in

Africa were reported in *Look* and in *Life*, and his home in Cuba was visited by the famous. Everyone talked of him . . . his books . . . his characters . . . his life.

Duke Ellington:
I learned from hearing his music that there was an immense poetry inside my life as an American Negro if I could find it.

Miles Davis, Thelonious Monk, Charlie Mingus:
Classical pervasive lyricism.

Philip Carey in OF HUMAN BONDAGE (Maugham):
He clarified the epic nature of human ups and downs. The human being must fight and struggle.

The original movie HUNCHBACK OF NOTRE DAME:
The power in fiction of the background of War.

All the people in the musical LOST IN THE STARS:
Especially Todd Duncan and Inez Matthews, who sang "Stay Well."

Chopin (again):
His études, scherzos, preludes and polonaises.

Puccini (LA BOHÈME):
Mimi, like Laura in *The Glass Menagerie*, became a self.

Langston Hughes:
His work defined a whole society of Negroes, and somehow in its power was defining and creating me personally.

Gene Kelly in SINGING IN THE RAIN:
When I had first seen *Singing in the Rain* (while at Ohio State) I had thought

how lucky Debbie Reynolds was that Gene Kelly fell in love with her as they danced together on the movie sound stage. Even now, when I was depressed I found myself singing "Singing in the Rain."

Sammy Davis, Jr.:
He defied categorization—an actor, singer and impersonator of actors and singers.

Katherine Dunham, Martha Graham:
Two women who inspired.

Grace Kelly:
Beauty, actress, princess. I envied her and her photographs in *Paris Match* standing in her gardens in Monaco, shopping in Paris, wearing dark glasses, being chased by paparazzi.

Harry Belafonte:
He was adored by everyone. The adoration crossed racial boundaries.

Hart Crane (poet):
He jumped off a ship. Why? I asked. Yet suicide would soon become a recurrent theme in my work.

Degas:
His lyricism.

Elizabeth Taylor:
Elizabeth Taylor in *A Place in the Sun*, Elizabeth Taylor in *Giant*, in *Cat on a Hot Tin Roof*. Elizabeth Taylor on the pages of *Look* and *Life*.

People in the MGM musicals:

Rossellini and Anna Magnani:

Brigitte Bardot:

Monet:
Color, density, texture of existence. I must learn how to translate these to paper and my stories.

Utrillo:
He made me pay closer attention (in his use of whites and perspective) to my dreams of white walls and disappearing figures and how I could use them in my writing.

Beethoven (again):
I bought a foot-high ivory statue of him at Pellenberg's on Broadway and put it on my desk for inspiration and read and reread Sullivan's book on the life of Beethoven—his spiritual development, his music, his lukewarm Danube baths and his growing deafness—and I listened to his string quartets.

Worthand Enders (THE NATURE OF LIVING THINGS):
Life cannot be defined precisely. Living things are familiar objects, but they may depend for their life on important dead components. . . . A book that helped me make new connections in the use of symbols in my work. Trying to learn to be specific in description, I studied the people in a book called *Art and Anatomy* and copied the highly specific description for practice.

Lorca (again):
After I read and saw *Blood Wedding,* I changed my ideas about what a play was. Ibsen, Chekhov, O'Neill and even Williams fell away. Never again would I try to set a play in a "living room," never again would I be afraid to have my characters talk in a nonrealistic way, and I would abandon the realistic set for a greater dream setting. It was a turning point.

Brooks Atkinson (NEW YORK TIMES theater critic):
I read every word he wrote on theater and what makes it excellent.

Martha Graham:
After I saw her production of *Clytemnestra,* the question of how I could use mythic characters in my own work grew in my mind.

Alfred Hitchcock (VERTIGO, 1958): *Vertigo* was perhaps the most influential movie of its time, in the impact it had on my imagination. Watching Kim Novak change identities was enthralling, and it was a contemporary story. I sensed there were elements in Hitchcock's use of the change of identities that, though still then closed off in my mind, might one day open up in my work.

Lorraine Hansberry:
I had abandoned playwriting by the time Lorraine Hansberry made her sensational entrance into the Broadway theater with the classic *A Raisin in the Sun*, because I thought there was no hope; but with Lorraine Hansberry's success, I felt reawakened. I read every word about her triumph and took heart.

Joanne Woodward:
Impassioned film actress, mother and wife, she seemed a miracle.

Diahann Carroll:
Richard Rodgers had written a Broadway musical for her. How in awe of this I was.

Emerson (again):
From his essay "Circles": "There are no fixtures in nature. The universe is fluid and volatile . . . nothing great was ever achieved without enthusiasm."
 In moments of despondency I read and reread Emerson.

Joseph K in Kafka's THE TRIAL:

Jack Kerouac's book THE SUBTERRANEANS:

Alain Delon:
In the Visconti movie *Rocco and His Brothers.*

People who soon would become characters in my plays:
Queen Victoria, Jesus, the Duchess of Hapsburg, Shakespeare, Chaucer, Patrice Lumumba, Anne Boleyn, the King of France and Chopin.

Some important people I'd forgotten:
>   Grace Metalious, author of *Peyton Place*
>   Diane Varsi, star of the movie *Peyton Place*
>   Helen Keller
>   Everyone at Birdland
>   Bing Crosby
>   Laurence Olivier (his eyes)
>   Thomas Mann (*Death in Venice*)
>   George Bernard Shaw (*Back to Methuselah*)
>   and Walt Disney

Eartha Kitt:
I thought her delightful and unique and, after all, Orson Welles (Edward Rochester) said she was the most beautiful woman in the world.

All these people:
I didn't know it at the time but all these people mingling in my life, my thoughts and my imagination were leading to a strengthening of my writing and a truer expression of it. All these people were presenting me with a form for my work as well as great inspiration.

I reread Charlotte Brontë (again):
She imbued in me a curiosity and love of the English moors which I would finally see twenty years later on a rainy, misty July afternoon when I would tour Haworth and the Brontës' house with the English poet Adrian Mitchell. No place had ever quite captured my imagination as wildly as Yorkshire, as the winding streets of Haworth.

110

I remembered—

Peggy Ann Garner in JANE EYRE:
She was the young Jane Eyre, cruelly treated by Aunt Reed and humiliated by the cruel Mr. Brocklehurst of the Lowood School. How I wanted to help her.

Miss D:
The mistress of our dormitory at Ohio State, a white-haired spinster with a cane, as hated in my mind as the cruel Mr. Brocklehurst of Lowood in *Jane Eyre*, a figure of authority to rebel, plot and dream against.

THE QUEEN MARY (1960):
My husband would soon take me on a miraculous voyage aboard the *Queen Mary* to England, France, Spain and West Africa. It would include an eight-month stay in Rome. This voyage played a crucial role in what was to follow in the next decade. I would begin to meet many more people and many whom I had dreamed of meeting.

A VOYAGE
1 9 6 0 – 1 9 6 1

On the QUEEN MARY
Africa
Georgia remembered
Julius Caesar
And pages that held a "destiny"

The ship QUEEN MARY, NOW,
   VOYAGER *and Bette Davis:*
In the fall of 1960, my husband
traveled to Africa to work. Our
whole family went with him. As
I stood on the deck of the *Queen
Mary* a morning in September
1960 thoughts of Bette Davis and
Now, Voyager flooded my mind.
At twenty-nine I felt defeated because I had not achieved my goal
to be a published writer. I vowed
as I stood on the deck and tug-
boats took us out into the Atlantic
that, like the character in *Now,
Voyager*, when I returned from
the journey I would be transformed . . . how or exactly in
what way transformed I didn't
know. Once into the voyage,
while my husband and son
roamed the ship I found some

beautiful paper from the ship's writing room, paper with a marvelous drawing of the *Queen Mary* at the top of each page, and I started a new story.

It would become the very first story I published—in *Black Orpheus*, a literary magazine edited by a German editor, Ulli Bieir, out of West Africa. The main character was based on my cousin who had run away to the Virgin Islands, and in my story had run away to the Virgin Islands *and* at the same time run away to France to live in Versailles.

Being on the ocean in these charming writing rooms (perhaps being on water) seemed to join the real and the unreal in my writing in a way that I had never before envisioned. This story, a brief one, was called "Because of the King of France" and it possessed a logic which had been evading me for a decade. The main character "behaved" in a certain way as a result of an encounter with the King of France, and with Chopin. It was a dramatic turning point in my work.

By the time we reached London, which would play a huge role in a play I would write in a few months, I was already seeing my work differently.

"Sidney," the character based on my cousin, had been a character I had worked on for at least three years. I had given him fantasies; but he had never taken "direct action" as a result of these fantasies. Now I began to dimly recognize that my statue of Beethoven that I kept on my desk as well as the photograph of Queen Hatshepsut were forces that caused me to act.

I remembered the miniature busts on Miss Eichenbaum's piano. Why had I not seen how real they were to me? How they caused me to behave differently? And here I was at twenty-nine compulsively trying to make myself a twin of Bette Davis in *Now, Voyager*, a movie I had seen at the Waldorf Theatre on a Saturday afternoon during World War II. The orange tower was still up then.

On the voyage:
Away from all my old books, but now besieged and surrounded by a myriad of real, astounding new imagery (ocean, staterooms, the decks, standing at the rail), my unconscious and conscious seemed to join in a new way.

116

I remembered—

Picasso's MADAME HÉLÈNE:
Often when I was depressed, my hair fell out, as my mother's hair fell out when I was born because of the ether she had to take during a difficult labor. At the Museum of Modern Art I had found a postcard of Picasso's *Madame Hélène*. Her hair seemed a living thing, an image I would soon use in my play *Funnyhouse of a Negro*.

Picasso's drawings of bullfights:
They showed the need for me to continue to try to achieve truth and power in very small sections of my stories and then analyze that success on a small scale.

David Duncan's pictures of Picasso at home in France:
On seeing photographs of Picasso sitting and walking amid large canvases and eating from plates decorated with his drawings of fish, I realized imagery in my work could take up a larger space. I was a person who after I wrote carefully stacked my pages and shut them inside the desk and closed the desk. More and more I tacked up on the wall cards, prints and photographs, even carried them with me. Finally I took to Scotch-taping my typewritten pages on the wall. It began to make a difference in my work.

Poe:
Many times I remembered "Annabel Lee," the poem I had recited to my sophomore English class in the spring of 1947. We were judged severely on our delivery, our diction, our interpretation of lines. Many nights I sat in my room with the blue wallpaper, or walked down the maple-tree-lined streets whispering over and over:

> "It was many and many a year ago,
>   In a Kingdom by the sea . . ."

All spring over and over, as I sat in the dining room across from my mother's china cabinets doing my homework, I repeated the lines. I wanted to be good. Perhaps it was then that I became aware of the power of repetition of lines of poetry, a device I would eventually use a great deal in my plays.

The Tower of London and Anne Boleyn (1960):
How fascinated by her I was as the Beefeater at the Tower of London told us how Henry VIII had imprisoned her, how she had walked the tower at night and how Henry had beheaded her. Soon Anne would become an image for imprisonment in a play, a confidante whom a character would discuss love and sorrow with.

The voyage:
As the Duchess of Hapsburg had haunted my mind, so would Queen Victoria come to do the same. The statue we saw of Victoria in front of Buckingham Palace was the single most dramatic, startling statue I'd seen. Here was a woman who had dominated an age.

In my play I would soon have the heroine, Sarah, talk to a replica of this statue. *Finally* the dialogue with a statue would be explicit and concrete. And the *statue* would reply; the *statue* would inform my character of her *inner* thoughts. The *statue* would reveal my character's secrets to herself.

Voyage:
Our family would soon see Cherbourg, the Tower of London, Trafalgar Square, Hyde Park, Versailles, the Opéra in Paris, the Louvre, the Tuilleries, the Sacré Coeur, the Seine, Madrid, the Prado, the streets and mosques of Casablanca, and fly into a sunset over Tunisia.

West Africa:
There where I saw the Ethiopian Princesses, the palace of Tubman, and the statue of Kwame Nkrumah, it was there I started the lines of two plays, *Funnyhouse of a Negro* and *The Owl Answers*, and the lines had a new power, a fierce new cadence.

Patrice Lumumba:
When we arrived in West Africa everyone talked of Patrice Lumumba, the Congo's young and heroic Prime Minister. And in Ghana, at every store and market, there were photographs of Lumumba walking with Kwame Nkrumah. (These men represented a vision of a freed Africa.) I carried the small gilt-edged photo of Nkrumah and Lumumba in my purse. Suddenly Lumumba was murdered.

"They killed Patrice Lumumba," everyone in the streets of Accra, in the restaurants, at the campus of Legon, said. "They've killed Patrice Lumumba. Lumumba was the hope."

Just when I had discovered the place of my ancestors, just when I had discovered this African hero, he had been murdered. Ghana was in mourning. There had been a deep kinship between Nkrumah and Lumumba. A few people we met had heard Lumumba speak. Even though I had known of him so briefly, I felt I had been struck a blow. He became a character in my play . . . a man with a shattered head.

My father and Patrice Lumumba:
I remembered my father's fine stirring speeches on the Negro cause . . . and Du Bois' articles in *Crisis* which my father had quoted. . . . There was

no doubt that Lumumba, this murdered hero, was merged in my mind with my father.

Tubman (President of Liberia):
He lived in a palace in the center of Monrovia. We stood outside the gates, just as we had stood outside the gates of Buckingham Palace, and looked beyond to the courtyards and palace. It was the first time I had seen a palace, an official palace, in which a Negro lived. A Black man living in a palace catapulted my consciousness onto a new level. A Black living in a palace and the President of a country . . . the idea of it made my blood rush. I had not seen the Ethiopian Princesses.

Ethiopian Princesses:
They sat on the terrace of the Ambassador Hotel in the sun drinking tea, wearing organza dresses. They had olive skin and opal-colored eyes. They're Ethiopian royalty . . . princesses, said the British man at the next table as everyone gazed at them.

Ulli Bieir (editor of BLACK ORPHEUS):
As soon as we arrived in Ghana I heard of a literary magazine, *Black Orpheus*, published by the German editor Ulli Bieir, who lived in Nigeria. On the journey to Ghana I had finished writing "Because of the King of France" and as soon as I saw a copy of the intriguing dark purple magazine with African drawings I decided to mail Bieir a copy of my story. In less than two weeks I received a letter from him saying:

> Dear Mrs. Kennedy:
> I like your story very much and would like to publish it in *Black Orpheus*.
> [An acceptance after more than ten years.]
> I will be in Accra in a few weeks and look forward to meeting you.

What happiness I felt as I sat in the yard of the Accra house. I reread the small transparent piece of paper over and over: "I would like to publish . . ."

When Ulli Bieir came to Accra, we all had dinner at the Achimota Guest

House and he invited us to Nigeria to meet his wife, a painter, who lived there. Word seemed to travel fast in West Africa among foreigners. It was soon known that I was having a story published in *Black Orpheus*. "Are you a writer?" people now asked. "Yes," I said. "Yes." I felt such exhilaration being published in *Black Orpheus* that I worked more feverishly on the passages and pages that I had started on the *Queen Elizabeth*.

We had stayed in several cities a week (London, Paris, Madrid, Casablanca) and in each city my notebook had filled up with ideas, thoughts, feelings, impressions. Now, after Joe had gone to the bush and our son had left for school on the campus of Legon, I worked constantly until one o'clock, when I walked to the school and picked him up.

The sun and the moon seemed to have a powerful effect on my senses. I felt on fire. We bought masks, cloth, musical instruments made of gourds, drove to the north of Ghana where men ran naked, drove to a village where vultures sat atop every tree, sat in a circle and sang with an African family, had tea with Ghanaian ambassadors in the lavish dining room of the Ambassador Hotel, and drove to the white beaches where wild white horses were running free.

Writers I read in Ghana:
Chinua Achebe, Amos Tutuola, Wole Soyinka, Eufua Sutherland, Lawrence Durrell (poems, especially one called "Christ in Brazil").

I bought these books at the bookstore at the University of Legon.

Now that I was going to be published in *Black Orpheus*, I was joined to these writers and I wanted to read their work.

Africans or the masks:
A few years before, Picasso's work had inspired me to exaggerate the physical appearances of my characters, but not until I bought a great African mask from a vendor on the streets of Accra, of a woman with a bird flying through her forehead, did I totally break from realistic-looking characters. I would soon create a character with a shattered, bludgeoned head. And that was his fixed surreal appearance.

The owls and myself:
The owls in the trees outside the Achimota Guest House were close, and at night, because we slept under gigantic mosquito nets, I felt enclosed in their

sound. In the mornings I would try to find the owls in the trees but could never see them. Yet, at night in the shuttered room, under the huge white canopied nets, the owls sounded as if they were in the very center of the room.

I was pregnant again. And there were difficulties. I had to stay in bed for a week, as I bled. I listened to the owl sounds, afraid. In a few months I would create a character who would turn into an owl.

Nkrumah:

In front of the House of Parliament in Accra was a statue of Nkrumah— often in the evenings we drove out into the savannahs to look at the compound in which his house sat and on Sundays we drove to the airport and watched Nkrumah arrive from trips. There would be ceremonies at which chieftains spoke. To see a man and to see a statue of him in the same space of time broke through boundaries in my mind. Statues were of real people.

Nkrumah's face:

His face was on cloth that was popular throughout Ghana: women made and wore dresses of it and men wore shirts of it. I bought as much as I could carry and made a skirt of the blue cloth with Nkrumah's face illustrated hugely in black and white. Because it had become a kind of national cloth, I felt when I wore it that I had sealed my ancestry as West African.

Myself:

The colors of Ghana caused me to remember my summers in Georgia . . . my grandparents . . . the landscape of Georgia. It all emerged in the passages I was writing.

My husband and myself:

I had never seen my husband less than I did now that we were in Africa. He left very early before daylight and was often in the bush two or three days. And now that I was pregnant, I would not be able to travel freely with him over Ghana. The doctor advised that I travel little until the fifth month of pregnancy. All of this produced growing tensions and unhappiness in me. It was now that I felt increasingly that I was just accompanying another person as he lived out his dreams. The long hours alone in the rented Accra home, at the guest house in Achimota or Kumasi, from dawn to late at night, filled me with fear. I was twenty-nine years old and a failure in my eyes. And although Africa had ignited a fire inside me and we looked forward to the birth of our second child, I felt (after being together for ten years) that I was acquiescent to another person's desires, dreams and hopes. The solitude under the African sun had brought out a darkness in me. I wanted to be more separate.

Jesus and my parents' marriage:

After much indecision my husband and I decided I would go to Italy and wait there until he finished his study in Nigeria. So there I was in the spring of 1961, the spring that my parents separated after thirty years of marriage. I received the letter from my mother (I'd walked down the Piazza di Spagna to American Express to get the mail) one May morning. The letter said they were separated, that my father no longer was living at home but was now in Georgia. I was not prepared for this shock. I could not envision my parents separate.

My mother had always said holding her family together was the most important thing in the world. Suddenly that spring Jesus became a character in the play I was writing, and a surprising Jesus, a punishing Jesus; berserk, evil, sinister.

I remembered how so long ago when we all took drives, when we had sat at the campfire together or listened to Jack Benny, I had seen Jesus as sweet, docile. I had believed "what a friend we have in Jesus." But that spring, sitting in the Pensione Sabrina, I went on creating a cruel Jesus Christ.

Mrs. Rosebaugh and Caesar:

Walking through the Roman Forum, I thought of Mrs. Rosebaugh and her stories of Caesar. I remembered the life of St. Augustine and how I studied the texture of his dialogue. I remembered copying the settings in Dante's *Purgatory*, I remembered that for three enchanting years I had sat in that Latin room, that pale-colored room, with the drawings of ancient Rome hung high on the wall.

And now, to see the Tiber, the Catacombs, to see the Hills of Rome, then I'd go back to the Pensione Sabrina and write.

My heroine, Sarah, would have photographs of Roman ruins in her room.

I remembered PHAEDRA *and how I studied dialogue:*

HIPPOLYTUS: *My mother was an Amazon . . . my wildness, which you think strange, I suckled at her breast,*
    And as I grew, why, Reason did approve what Nature planted in me.
    Then you told me the story of my father and you know how often when I listened to your voice I kindled hearing of his noble acts.

The length of the monologues, as well as the context, was very influential.

Our family:
Joe arrived from West Africa the week before the birth of our son Adam. How thrilling it was for us sitting in the garden of the Salvator Mundi Hospital with our new baby. We remained in Rome for six weeks . . . strolling on the Via Veneto . . . in the Villa Borghese . . . eating dinner in sidewalk cafés . . . our lives seemed perfect.

Adam, our son born in Salvator Mundi Hospital (on the Janiculum Hill):
His birth brought into focus the need for me to understand where I stood in relationship to my work. I knew I faced two years when caring for a small child was exhausting. I thought, I am never going to write another word now. I have this short play that I have finished. When I return to New York, I will send it around. If no one accepts it, I will totally give

up my writing; my husband is successful. We have two sons and for ten years I have struggled. While I had been in Africa I had sent part of a story to my agent at MCA and he had written back that he no longer thought he could do anything with my work.

Our son Adam:
His middle name was Patrice.

Myself:
We sailed back to New York on the *United States*. I had a completed play in my suitcase. How could I know it would establish me as a playwright and change my life? After years of writing, I had finally written of myself and my family and it would be on stage and in a book too, and I would be on the pages of *Vogue* and in Leonard Lyons' column.

And in a few months I would climb the steps to the Circle in the Square theater where I would see this play inside my suitcase performed, become a member of the Actors Studio (where Brando had been) and become a part of the Off-Broadway theater movement . . . a movement that in itself would come to occupy a powerful place in American theater history.

PERMISSIONS ACKNOWLEDGMENTS

Grateful acknowledgment is made to the following for permission
to reproduce illustrations on the pages indicated:

page

3	Courtesy Dover Publications
4	Courtesy The Granger Collection, New York
8	Courtesy The Granger Collection, New York
14	Courtesy The Granger Collection, New York
15	Courtesy The Bettmann Archive
17	Courtesy The Memory Shop, New York
18	Courtesy Pictorial Parade
19	Courtesy The Granger Collection, New York
	Courtesy Culver Pictures, New York
21	Copyright © 1937 The Walt Disney Company
24	Courtesy The Memory Shop, New York
25	Courtesy The Granger Collection, New York
26	Courtesy The Museum of Modern Art Film Stills Archive
27	Courtesy John Toland; copyright © Dr. Schultze
33	Courtesy The Granger Collection, New York
41	Copyright © Philippe Halsman
46	Courtesy The Bettmann Archive
47	Courtesy The Bettmann Archive
61	Courtesy The Kobal Collection
70	Courtesy Wide World Photos, New York
87	Courtesy The Granger Collection, New York
91	Courtesy Bibliothèque Nationale, Paris
95	Courtesy Magnum Photos, New York
	Courtesy The Memory Shop, New York
	Courtesy The Bettmann Archive
	Courtesy The Granger Collection, New York
96	Reprinted with permission of Macmillan Publishing Co. from *The World's Great Men of Color*, Volume One, by J. A. Rogers, copyright 1946 Helga M. Rogers, renewed 1974; copyright © 1972 Macmillan Publishing Co.

page

99   Courtesy The Granger Collection, New York
       Courtesy The Bettmann Archive
       Courtesy of Daphne Du Maurier
104   Courtesy The Granger Collection, New York
106   Courtesy The Granger Collection, New York
109   Courtesy The Estate of Ruth Orkin
115   Courtesy Cunard Archives, Liverpool
118   Courtesy The Granger Collection, New York
125   Courtesy of Steelograph, New York

ADRIENNE KENNEDY has been a force in the American theatre since the early 1960s, influencing generations of playwrights with her hauntingly fragmentary lyrical dramas. Exploring the violence that racism visits upon people's lives, her plays express poetic alienation, transcending the particulars of character and plot through ritualistic repetition and radical structural experimentation. Frequently produced, read and taught, Kennedy's works continue to hold a significant place among the most exciting dramas of the past fifty years.

Ms. Kennedy is a three-time Obie Award–winning playwright, receiving awards for *Funnyhouse of a Negro* in 1964 and *June and Jean in Concert* in 1996. She has received numerous honors, including the American Academy of Arts and Letters Award for Literature, The Anisfield-Wolf Book Award for Lifetime Achievement and a Guggenheim fellowship. She has been commissioned to write works for The Public Theater, Jerome Robbins, the Royal Court Theatre, the Mark Taper Forum and Juilliard. In 1995–96, the Signature Theatre Company dedicated its entire season to presenting her works.

Ms. Kennedy has been a visiting professor at Yale, Princeton, Brown, the University of California at Berkeley, and ended her teaching career with six semesters at Harvard. She resides in New York City.